5

Things You Can Do To
UNDERSTAND
THE BIBLE
BETTER

ZACH MCINTOSH

CONCORDIA PUBLISHING HOUSE · SAINT LOUIS

For Melody, my beloved wife:

While I teach the Word, you support me
with the Word in your words and deeds.

Copyright © 2013 Concordia Publishing House
3558 S. Jefferson Avenue, St. Louis, MO 63118-3968
1-800-325-3040 • www.cph.org

Scripture quotations are from the ESV Bible® (The Holy Bible, English Standard Version®), copyright © 2001 by Crossway Bibles, a publishing ministry of Good News Publishers. Used by permission. All rights reserved.

Hymn texts with the abbreviation *LSB* are from *Lutheran Service Book*, copyright © 2006 Concordia Publishing House. All rights reserved.

The quotations from Martin Luther are taken from *Luther's Small Catechism with Explanation*, copyright © 1986, 1991 Concordia Publishing House. All rights reserved.

What Luther Says: A Practical In-Home Anthology for the Active Christian, ed. Ewald M. Plass, copyright © 1959 Concordia Publishing House. All rights reserved.

The quotations from *Luther's Works* in this publication are from *Luther's Works, American Edition* (56 vols.; St. Louis: Concordia Publishing House and Philadelphia: Fortress Press, 1955–86).

The quotations from the Lutheran Confessions in this publication are from *Concordia: The Lutheran Confessions*, second edition; edited by Paul McCain, et al., copyright © 2006 Concordia Publishing House. All rights reserved.

Excerpts from *The God Delusion* by Richard Dawkins. Copyright © 2006 by Richard Dawkins. Used by permission of Houghton Mifflin Harcourt Publishing Company. All rights reserved.

Manufactured in the United States of America

1   2   3   4   5   6   7   8   9   10   22   21   20   19   18   17   16   15   14   13

TABLE OF CONTENTS

It is the best-selling book of all time. In fact, regardless of what is on the *New York Times* Best Seller list, it is probably the best-selling book of this week. Because it is published in so many different languages by so many different publishers, its sales numbers are impossible to track. The book is the Bible. And there is simply no other book like it—not in its contents, not in its popularity, not in the hope and comfort it offers, and not in its origin.

Recently, the King James Version of the Bible celebrated its four hundredth anniversary. In 1604, King James I of England commissioned a group of theologians to translate the Bible from its original languages of Hebrew, Aramaic, and Greek into English. An earlier English translation, the Bishops' Bible, was too linguistically cumbersome and complicated to be read and understood, much less enjoyed, by the masses. King James wanted to change that. That royal commission bore fruit in 1611 in what came to be known as the King James Bible. To mark the anniversary, *National Geographic* published a cover story on both the history of the King James Bible and its effects on the English language.[1] The story cited some of its phrases, so worn with use that many have no clue as to their origins:

> Keep me as the apple of the eye, hide me under the shadow of Thy wings. (Psalm 17:8)
>
> They reel to and fro, and stagger like a drunken man, and are at their wit's end. (Psalm 107:27)

Let them alone: they be blind leaders of the blind.
And if the blind lead the blind, both shall fall
into the ditch. (Matthew 15:14)

My bone cleaveth to my skin and to my flesh, and
I am escaped with the skin of my teeth. (Job 19:20)

Whether or not we are aware of it, the Bible has profoundly shaped our speaking and our language. Its pervasiveness is inescapable. Yet, as popular as the Bible's famous phrases and favorite verses may be, many people—even Christians—are largely unfamiliar with its broader contents and its joyous, even if sometimes austere, theology.

The statistics tell the story. A 2007 *Time* magazine article noted that only half of adults in the United States could name one of the four Gospels. Fewer than half knew that Genesis was the Bible's first book. Meanwhile, in other polls, 82 percent of Americans believed the phrase "God helps those who help themselves" was a biblical one. Finally, in a truly grinworthy statistic, 12 percent of adults thought that Noah's wife was Joan of Arc. The Bible may be the best-selling book of all time, but for all its sales, it remains widely unopened.

Therefore, *5 Things You Can Do to Understand the Bible Better* will not simply give you another to-do list but will encourage you to do the one thing that helps in understanding the Bible better than anything else: read it! For a world that knows little more about the Bible than its famous "sound bites"—phrases ripped from their respective histories and contexts—I will provide a broad overview of the most beloved and most criticized book. I will also try to answer some of the common questions and objections that people have concerning the Bible. This overview, of course, will in no way be exhaustive, nor is it meant to be. But as more people become unfamiliar with and hostile toward Holy Scripture, this book will arm the interested reader with at least a basic knowledge of the purposes and themes of the Bible.

Most important, you'll come to know the Bible as God wants it understood: as a gripping account of His saving work among human beings through the person of Jesus Christ. Jesus is Scripture's central character and message. Without Him, the Bible would offer no hope, no comfort, and no salvation. But with Jesus, the Bible offers all these things. Through Jesus, God is changing lives and saving them. And that's what this book, the Bible, is all about. That's why it really is the Good Book.

1

My wife's favorite show, *Wheel of Fortune,* is appointment television in our household. Its enduring popularity is thanks in part to the show's longtime, amicable hosts, Pat Sajak and Vanna White. For over thirty years, these two have been so integral to the *Wheel of Fortune* enterprise that, for many seasons, Sajak and White weren't referred to as the show's "hosts" but as the show's "stars." Whenever the announcer would introduce them, the audience would instantly erupt in applause. The show centers around its stars at least as much as it does its puzzle board, prizes, or even contestants.

The Star of Scripture

Just as *Wheel of Fortune* has two stars who feature prominently in everything about the show, the Bible has a star who features prominently in all it has to say: Jesus Christ. Though this may seem self-evident to some, it is readily forgotten by many. As a result, the Bible is often misread and misused. Progressive readers regularly treat the Bible as if it's nothing more than a collection of mythical stories with lofty moral aspirations, much akin to Aesop's Fables. It then becomes the job of the reader to cull from the many myths of Scripture kernels of moral truth, which, coincidently enough, seem to mirror the broader sentiments and sensitivities of society. Along the way the progressive reader discards the inconsequential husks of history and divine mandates that offend the prevailing public opinion.

For more traditional readers, the Bible is often treated as a comprehensive instruction book outlining how to live a pious and noble life. Some even propose that such a biblically conscientious life can lead a person into eternal bliss, as the old acronym B-I-B-L-E intimates: "Basic Instructions Before Leaving Earth." Though people of this second persuasion may believe the Bible to be more true and less mythical than those of the progressive persuasion, both groups treat the Bible in essentially the same way: as a moral handbook, good for giving its reader a laundry list of dos and don'ts for clean living. They do not, however, recognize the contents of Scripture as a drama of divine intervention, revealing God's rescue plan of Jesus to a world trapped in sin and death. Such readers, therefore, misread and misuse Scripture, for they read the Bible in a way that does not keep Jesus at the center.

Scripture stars Jesus Christ. Jesus Himself says so: "The Scriptures . . . bear witness about Me" (John 5:39). And though the New Testament is where His life, ministry, death, and resurrection are chronicled, Jesus clarifies that He is the star of the Old Testament as well. When the religious leaders of His day boast about their ritual rigor with regard to the Mosaic Law, Jesus responds, "If you believed Moses, you would believe Me; for he wrote of Me" (John 5:46). Jesus sees the story of Moses—from the Israelite exodus out of slavery in Egypt to their trek into the Promised Land—as a microcosm of His own work and ministry, for He has come to lead people out of their slavery to sin and into the promised land of eternity (Luke 9:30–31). Moses' story is really Jesus' story. Jesus speaks similarly to His own followers when, after His death and resurrection, they become bemused by all that has happened. To clear away the theological cobwebs, Jesus opens the Old Testament and "beginning with Moses and all the Prophets, He interpreted to them in all the Scriptures the things concerning Himself" (Luke 24:27). Everything in the Bible—from Moses to the Prophets, from the historical narratives of Samuel and Kings to the poetry of the Psalms, from the birth of the Church in Acts to the promise of a new creation in Revelation—points to Jesus. Martin Luther explains it succinctly: "All stories in Holy Scripture refer to Christ."[1] Scripture stars Jesus Christ.

But Jesus is more than just the star of the Bible. He plays all the supporting roles as well. Many times, pastors and Christian authors speak of biblical heroes—folks like Abraham or Samson or David—who, thanks to their bold faith, superhuman strength, or victories in battle, are held up as righteous paragons worthy of emulation. While there are lessons to be gleaned from these saints, one does not have to scrape hard to remove the thin gild of heroism that has been sloppily overlaid on these biblical personalities throughout the millennia. Abraham was a liar (Genesis 12:10–20). Samson was a womanizer (Judges 16:1). David was an adulterer and a murderer (2 Samuel 12:9). The shockingly sinful lives of these so-called biblical heroes compel us to conclude that the positive lessons to be learned from these ancients are based not

To learn more about Jesus as the "star" of all Scripture, read "The Word and the Word Made Flesh" in *The Lutheran Difference*, Edward A. Engelbrecht, ed., (Concordia, 2010), pp. 31–38.

on the inherent righteousness in their characters but on the grace of Christ in their lives. The preacher of Hebrews reminds us, "The Lord is my helper" (13:6). The Lord was clearly a helper to these sinners of old, salvaging their broken lives and shattered reputations for His glory and for their benefit. The Lord is our helper too.

The Inspiration of Scripture

Jesus is also Scripture's screenwriter. In other words, along with the Father and the Holy Spirit, He is the author of the very book in which He stars. In a passage familiar to many, the apostle Paul writes to a young pastor named Timothy concerning Scripture's divine origin: "All Scripture is breathed out by God and profitable for teaching, for reproof, for correction, and for training in righteousness, that the man of God may be complete, equipped for every good work" (2 Timothy 3:16–17). Here, Paul outlines for Timothy the doctrine of inspiration, asserting that the Bible finds its origin and authority in God Himself.

That Scripture is divinely inspired is nothing new. Divine inspiration cannot be chalked up to some sort of modern-era fundamentalism that desires to wield the Bible as a holy club, beating the masses into submission until it can usher in a theocratic utopia. Clement, a first-century bishop at Rome, wrote in a letter to the Christian Church at Corinth: "Take up the epistle of the blessed apostle Paul. What did he write to you at the time when the Gospel first began to be preached? Truly, under the inspiration of the Spirit, he wrote to you concerning himself."[2] Clement asserts that Paul's letters to the Corinthian Christians are really the Spirit's letters to the Corinthian Christians. Paul's letters find their source and force in the Holy Spirit.

Luther also held Scripture to be divinely authored: "No book, teaching, or word is able to comfort in troubles, fear, misery, death, yea, in the midst of devils and in hell, except this book, which teaches us God's Word and in which God Himself speaks with us as a man speaks with his friend."[3] If you want to hear God speak, Luther says, open your Bible.

When speaking of the inspiration of Scripture, it is helpful to apply three adjectives to this doctrine to clarify what is being confessed.

VERBAL To say that Scripture is verbally inspired is to say that God orchestrated Scripture's very verbs, or words, and not just its general thoughts, concepts, or ideas. Thus, every word of the Bible is important. Jesus asserts this very thing when He declares, "Do not think that I have come to abolish the Law or the Prophets; I have not come to abolish them but to fulfill them. For truly, I say to you, until heaven and earth pass away, not an iota, not a dot, will pass from the Law until all is accomplished" (Matthew 5:17–18). Jesus' reference to "iotas" and "dots" is especially forceful. An "iota" refers to the Hebrew letter *yod*, the smallest letter in the Hebrew alphabet. A "dot" describes the hooks and lines on serif fonts, of which Hebrew script has plenty. Thus, when Jesus says, "Not an iota, not a dot, will pass from the Law," He is saying that not only is it vital to have a high regard for the very words of Scripture, one must consider even the tiniest letters, yes, even the tiniest strokes on the tiniest letters, as essential to the integrity of the biblical text. It is difficult to imagine a higher view of Scripture than this! This is what is meant by verbal inspiration.

PLENARY "Plenary" is from the Latin word *plenus*, meaning "full" or "complete." Thus, when we speak of the plenary inspiration of Scripture, we are saying that God inspires all of the Bible, and not just parts of it: "All Scripture is breathed out by God" (2 Timothy 3:16). Plenary inspiration is especially important in a day and age when many people feel at liberty to pick and choose which parts of the Bible they will believe and follow. Claims abound that certain parts of Scripture are no longer relevant or are culturally conditioned. For instance, the Bible's teaching on human sexuality and its admonition that sexual intimacy is to be expressed only within the confines and context of marriage (Hebrews 13:4) is often breezily dismissed as outdated prudishness passed down to us as part of the ethical restrictions of the Victorian era, even though the New Testament, from which the Christian standards on sexuality are drawn, was written some nineteen centuries before the dawn of that era! Such a dismissal seems to be more the product of a flippant disobedience to Scripture in the interest of pursuing one's own passions rather than a thoughtful inquiry into the scope of the authority of

Scripture. Plenary inspiration clarifies that a person cannot dismiss certain scriptural teachings, such as the Bible's teaching on human sexuality, at will and at whim. To believe that Scripture is inspired by God is to believe that all of Scripture is inspired by God.

INERRANT The connection between Scripture's inspiration and its inerrancy is straightforward: to believe that God inspired the very words of the Bible in their totality, one must also believe that the human authors recorded those very words of God without error. To assert otherwise would mean that God, the Perfect and Holy One, is capable of imperfection and can make a mistake. The Bible lays claim to its own inerrancy in places such as Psalm 19:7: "The law of the LORD is perfect, reviving the soul; the testimony of the LORD is sure, making wise the simple." The Word of the Lord, the psalmist declares, is "perfect." Perfection leaves no room for error.

The Trustworthiness of Scripture

Claims concerning the Bible's inspiration—especially those made by the Bible itself—are understandably met with a fair amount of skepticism. After all, asserting a truth on the basis of claims that a thing makes about itself is circular reasoning, a logical fallacy. Blessedly, the Bible demonstrates its inspiration and trustworthiness in other ways. Here are additional reasons, apart from the Bible's own claims, why you can trust that the Bible is what it says it is.

YOU CAN TRUST THE BIBLE
BECAUSE IT HAS BEEN REPEATEDLY SHOWN
TO BE HONEST IN ITS PRESENTATION OF FACTS.

There has been no shortage of attempts to undermine the historical credibility of the Bible. Take Luke's renowned account of the Christmas story:

> In those days a decree went out from Caesar Augustus that all the world should be registered. This was the first registration when Quirinius was governor of Syria. And all went to be registered, each to his own town. And Joseph also went up from Galilee, from the town of Nazareth, to Judea, to the city of David, which is called Bethlehem, because he was of the house and lineage of David, to be registered with Mary, his betrothed, who was with child. (Luke 2:1–5)

For years, skeptics, giddy at the specter of undercutting the Bible's authority, ridiculed the notion that a whole empire full of people would have to return to their towns of origin to be registered in a census. After all, how could a kingdom as large as Rome's shuffle so many people back to their birthplaces? Joseph and Mary's journey to Bethlehem for a census was panned as utter fiction, that is, until just such an edict was found from AD 104 demanding Egyptians under Roman rule return to the towns of their origins to be registered in a census. All of a sudden, the scoffs of the skeptics crumbled under the weight of the historical record. Luke had it right all along.

Or how about the protestations against the prophecies of Daniel? Because this apocalyptic masterstroke contains many predictions that, with uncanny precision, came to pass over the next five centuries, skeptics once insisted that these prophecies weren't prophecies after all, that they had to have been written after the fact. According to these cynics, Daniel's premonitions were really only descriptions of what had already happened dressed in prophetic garb to make them appear as though they were spoken before the events they record. One can imagine the skeptics' shock when it was discovered that the Jewish community at Qumran held Daniel and his prophecies to be part of the Bible as early as 171 BC, before the balance of the prophecies of the book had even been fulfilled! Daniel, guided by the Holy Spirit, had the ability to predict the future after all. Again, Scripture's claims about itself turned out to be reliable.

YOU CAN TRUST THE BIBLE
BECAUSE IT IS A HIGHLY UNLIKELY BOOK.

One of the ways to spot historical forgery in an autobiography is to look for self-aggrandizing statements. Such statements are meant to impress the reader with the skill and intellect of their author because the author has a vested interest in how he presents himself. The Gospels, even if they are not autobiographical in the strictest sense, certainly have autobiographical elements. Matthew was one of Jesus' twelve apostles. Mark was most probably written with the apostle Peter's help. Luke was a friend of the disciples. And John was part of Jesus' inner circle. Thus, each of the Gospels could have easily been written as propaganda pieces for the disciples, highlighting their faith and faithfulness to Jesus. But the Gospels contain no such self-promotion. Instead, the disciples are consistently presented as unable to comprehend even the most basic teachings of Christ. After Jesus tells the parable of the sower, He has to interpret it for His disciples because they do not understand it (Mark 4:13–20). When Jesus predicts His death and resurrection, Mark notes that the disciples "did not understand the saying, and were afraid to ask Him" (Mark 9:32). Even at the close of Jesus' earthly ministry, after He had poured some three years into His disciples, mentoring them and teaching them that His kingdom is "not of this world" (John 18:36), His disciples ask Him, right before His ascension, "Lord, will You at this time restore the kingdom to Israel?" (Acts 1:6). The disciples are still looking for a rebel leader to drive out the Romans and restore sovereignty to the nation of Israel even though Jesus has made it abundantly clear that His mission is one of salvation and not revolution. The disciples, it seems, are pitifully slow to understand. Yet, the disciples' denseness is not glossed over by their close associates, or even by the disciples themselves, in the Gospel accounts. There is no self-aggrandizement here.

Similar to this is the priority the disciples give themselves in the Gospels. One would think that in a Gospel written by Matthew, the apostle would seek to draw attention to himself as one of the Twelve. But he does not. In his own Gospel, he mentions himself only twice (Matthew 9:9; 10:3). Likewise, John is so shy he doesn't even refer to himself by name in his Gospel, instead calling himself "the disciple whom Jesus loved" (see John 19:26; 20:2; 21:7).

Clearly, the priority of the people who wrote the Gospels in particular and the Bible in general was not themselves. Instead, the scriptural authors were willing to air their personal dirty laundry, no matter how embarrassing, in order to tell the truth about Jesus. If they were willing to do that, perhaps we should believe what they say.

YOU CAN TRUST THE BIBLE
ON ACCOUNT OF THE UNITY OF ITS MESSAGE.

C. F. W. Walther summarizes the unity of the Bible's message this way: "The doctrinal contents of all Holy Scripture, both of the Old and the New Testament, consist of two doctrines that differ fundamentally from each other. These two doctrines are Law and Gospel."[4] Walther says that one way the Scriptures speak to us is through the Law. The Law "shows, reproves, and condemns sins" (Apology XIIA 53). In other words, the Law convicts us of our sin and shows us that we need salvation from sin. The Gospel, on the other hand, brings us the salvation we need through the forgiveness that comes from Christ (Acts 13:38–39). Thus, the Law, in its condemnation of our sin, leads us to Christ so that we may receive and believe the Gospel—the forgiveness of our sin. Law and Gospel: these are the two great doctrines of the Bible, and both are grounded in Christ (Galatians 3:24–26). Many have marveled at the fact that though the Bible was written over a period of some fifteen hundred years in three different languages by more than forty different human authors, it has a remarkably unified message. It consistently tells of a God who works relentlessly to save His people. Jesus is the way He does this, which means the Bible is all about Jesus. If you remember nothing else from this book, remember that.

To read more about the inspiration and authority of Scripture, read *Light from Above* by Alfred W. Koehler (Concordia, 2012), pp 17–19, and "Now That's Inspired" in *The Lutheran Difference*, pp. 10–18.

Key Points

- You will not read the Bible well unless you see Christ as its center.

- It's not just the New Testament that features Jesus; the Old Testament points to Him as well.

- In addition to being the center of Scripture, Jesus is its author.

- Scripture's divine authorship is regularly referred to as verbal, plenary, and inerrant inspiration.

- The trustworthiness of Scripture is both internally and externally proven.

- Scripture is unified under two doctrines: Law and Gospel. The Law shows us our sins. The Gospel points us to our Savior.

Discussion Questions

1. The Bible is all about Jesus! How can this simple truth help you read the Bible differently? Do you ever have a difficult time relating a passage or a story to Jesus? Give some examples. Where can you turn for help?

2. Read Genesis 22:1–14 and consider how the following passages relate to Christ:

   VERSE 2: "Take your son, your only son Isaac, whom you love, and go to the land of Moriah, and offer him there as a burnt offering on one of the mountains of which I shall tell you." (See John 3:16.)

   VERSE 6: "And Abraham took the wood of the burnt offering and laid it on Isaac his son." (See John 19:17.)

   VERSE 13: "Abraham went and took the ram and offered it up as a burnt offering instead of his son." (See Hebrews 10:11–18.)

3. Can you think of an instance where a Christian author or speaker has treated the Bible as a moral handbook rather the revelation of God's intervention in Christ?

How can an understanding of Scripture that is centered in Christ help you discern what is true from what is false as you read or listen to these people?

4. Because Christ is the author of the Bible and He does not lie, it is a totally true book. Are there any passages or parts of Scripture that you have a hard time believing? What makes these passages difficult to believe? Where can you turn to better understand these difficult passages?

Action Items

1. As you read the Bible, highlight the Christ-specific passages with a star in the margin to remind you that Scripture stars Jesus Christ.

2. Law and Gospel are not only doctrines in Scripture, but they are also the ways by which Christians live. In what ways are Law and Gospel needed . . .

   . . . in your marriage?

   . . . in your parenting?

   . . . at your job?

3. Are there any areas or ways in which you can grow in distinguishing Law and Gospel? Note these areas and ways and seek to improve!

4. The next time you listen to a sermon or attend a Bible study, keep track of how the pastor or teacher relates what is being proclaimed or studied to Christ.

5. Write down your toughest question about the Bible's truthfulness or authenticity. Discuss it with your pastor in Bible class or one-on-one.

Schlotzsky's is a nationally known deli-style sandwich shop. The advertising slogan they used when I was in college pretty much sums up the reason for their success: "Schlotzsky's. Funny name. Serious sandwich."

TaNaKh. Funny name. Serious substance.

In Hebrew, the Old Testament is called the *TaNaKh*. My spell-check doesn't like that word either. It's a funny name. But even with its funny name, the *TaNaKh* presents its reader with some serious theological substance.

Each of the capital letters in the word *TaNaKh* stands for one of the three main divisions of the Old Testament.

The T stands for *Torah*, often translated "law." The Torah covers the first five books of the Bible, written by Moses: Genesis, Exodus, Leviticus, Numbers, and Deuteronomy. The translation of Torah as "law" is unfortunate. For in the Torah, God does much more than mete out sacred statutes. He instructs His people, teaching them about Himself while promising to love them steadfastly (Deuteronomy 7:9). This is why Torah can be better translated as "instruction."

The N stands for *Nebi'im*, the Hebrew word for "Prophets." This section includes the former prophets of Joshua, Judges, the two books of Samuel, and the two books of Kings. There are also the so-called major prophets of Isaiah, Jeremiah, Ezekiel, and Daniel as well as the so-called minor prophets of Hosea, Joel, Amos, Obadiah, Jonah, Micah, Nahum, Habakkuk, Zephaniah, Haggai, Zechariah, and Malachi.

These prophets are called minor, not because their message is less important, but because their books are shorter than those of the major prophets.

Finally, the *K* stands for *Ketubim*, the Hebrew word for "Writings." The Writings of the Old Testament cover the gamut of literary genres—from historical narratives in Ezra, Nehemiah, and the two books of Chronicles to poetry in the Psalms to wisdom literature in Proverbs and Ecclesiastes.

It's worth it to unpack each of these Old Testament sections.

T **is for** *Torah*

Out of all the sections of the Old Testament, the Torah held primacy of place for the ancient Jews. Jewish oral tradition claimed that a person who did not believe the Torah came from heaven would have no share in the world to come. No Torah, no salvation. This is how seriously the ancient Jews took the Torah.

Part of the reason the Torah was so revered is because it told of Israel's and of the world's origin. The Hebrew name for the account of the beginning is *Bereshith*, meaning "In the beginning," or as we know it, "Genesis." In the opening chapters of Genesis, we read the complementary accounts of the beginning of the world and, specifically, about the creation of humankind. In chapter 3, things take a turn for the worse when the first two humans, Adam and Eve, rebel against God and bring sin into the world. From chapter 3 forward, things go downhill quickly. Adam and Eve have two sons, Cain and Abel. In a fit of jealous rage, Cain kills his brother (4:1–16). The subsequent descendants of Adam and Eve are so exceedingly wicked that by the time of Genesis 6, God has had enough:

> The LORD saw that the wickedness of man was
> great in the earth, and that every intention of
> the thoughts of his heart was only evil continually.
> And the LORD regretted that He had made man
> on the earth, and it grieved Him to His heart.
> So the LORD said, "I will blot out man whom I have
> created from the face of the land, man and animals
> and creeping things and birds of the heavens,
> for I am sorry that I have made them." (vv. 5–7)

God's response to the corruption of sin is terrible wrath. He sends a worldwide flood, rescuing only Noah, his family, and some animals via an ark. But even God's catastrophic judgment does not stem the tide of human wickedness. By Genesis 11, humans are back to their old tricks, this time trying to assert their supremacy over God by building a tower to the skies. God responds by confusing their language so they cannot communicate with one another and complete their bombastic building project.

It is in the midst of all this human iniquity that God aims to make a new beginning. He calls a man named Abram, changes his name to Abraham, and makes him two promises.

First, God promises Abraham, "I will make of you a great nation" (Genesis 12:2). And God does. Abraham becomes the father of the nation of Israel. Second, God promises, "In you all the families of the earth shall be blessed" (v. 3). God desires that Abraham and his descendants be beacons of blessing in a world filled with rampant sinfulness. But Abraham's descendants do not fair so well at carrying out God's commission. Rather than sharing God's blessing, Abraham's descendants join in the world's rebellion.

We see an example of this rebellion when, over six hundred years after God calls Abraham, his descendants, the Israelites, are stuck in Egypt, commandeered as slave labor for the Pharaoh of that day. To rescue His people from their oppressors, God raises up Moses to lead His people out from Egypt and into freedom. The Israelites, after centuries of subjugation, are finally free. So how do they thank God for emancipating them? They grumble.

> The whole congregation of the people of Israel grumbled against Moses and Aaron in the wilderness. (Exodus 16:2)

> The people thirsted there for water, and the people grumbled against Moses. (Exodus 17:3)

> All the people of Israel grumbled against Moses and Aaron. The whole congregation said to them, "Would that we had died in the land of Egypt! Or would that we had died in this wilderness!" (Numbers 14:2)

Again and again, the Israelites grumble about their liberation, going so far as to say, "Would that we had died by the hand of the LORD in the land of Egypt, when we sat by the meat pots and ate bread to the full" (Exodus 16:3). The Israelites prefer their slavery in Egypt to freedom as the people of God.

It's not as if God doesn't give the Israelites opportunities to get back on the right track. He comforts them with His presence using a pillar of cloud by day and a pillar of fire by night (Exodus 13:17–22). He miraculously parts the Red Sea for them so they can witness His power and learn to trust His providence (ch. 14). He feeds them with plentiful quail and mysterious bread from heaven in the midst of the barren desert through which they traveled (ch. 16). He methodically details for them the way He desired them to live, a way that would define and mark them as the chosen nation of God, not only through the renowned Ten Commandments, but through His levitical laws.

Unfortunately, the laws in Leviticus have become a flashpoint for many questions and objections. These laws range from the widely venerated "You shall love your neighbor as yourself" (19:18) to the perplexing "Nor shall you wear a garment of cloth made of two kinds of material" (19:19). Loving your neighbor is "in" according to these laws. Your polyester/cotton T-shirt, however, is "out."

With such a wide array of levitical laws, it can be difficult to sort through what is what. Why do we still demand that we love our neighbors while feeling free to do so in a polyester/cotton T-shirt? Part of the answer can be found in the types of laws given in Scripture. Theologians have often distinguished between three types of Old Testament laws.

CIVIL LAWS. Civil laws were given by God to order life in the ancient nation of Israel. These include everything from particular punishments for various crimes, such as capital punishment in the case of murder (e.g., Leviticus 24:17), to health regulations for the safety of the Israelites, such as the burning of fabrics that become contaminated (e.g., 13:47–52). Because these laws are civic in nature and were thus for the ancient Israelites specifically, they are not to be followed, nor were they intended to be followed, by all nations generally. The apostle Paul notes that national leaders are free to govern as they see fit as long as their governance promotes society's general welfare (Romans 13:1–7). Jesus Himself jettisons many of Israel's civil penalties, such as that of execution for the crime of adultery, knowing that such civic penalties, especially as arbitrarily and hypocritically applied by the religious leaders of His day, are not incumbent on His ministry of grace (John 8:2–11; Deuteronomy 22:23–24). Likewise, the Church is under no compulsion to follow Old Testament civil laws. After all, the Church is not a political body whose order is tied to the civics of ancient Israel but an organic body of believers whose mission is salvific. This is why the Church deals with sin, even with a heinous sin like murder, by confession and forgiveness (James 5:16) rather than by capital punishment.

SACRIFICIAL AND CEREMONIAL LAWS. These include everything from the slaughtering of goats for the sins of Israel (Leviticus 16:15–16) to the many stipulations surrounding the care of the tabernacle and, later, of the temple (e.g., 24:1–9). The preacher of Hebrews tells us why the sacrificial and ceremonial laws are no longer implemented in the Church: "Every priest stands daily at his service, offering repeatedly the same sacrifices, which can never take away sins. But when Christ had offered for all time a single sacrifice for sins, He sat down at the right hand of God" (10:11–12). Because of Christ's perfect sacrifice on the cross, we no longer need lesser levitical sacrifices performed by priests, nor do we need the place at which these sacrifices were offered: the temple. The curtain of the temple was torn in two upon Jesus' death to mark the end of such sacrifices (Matthew 27:51).

MORAL LAWS. The moral laws include everything from concern for the physically challenged—"You shall not curse the deaf or put a stumbling block before the blind" (Leviticus 19:14)—to prohibitions against hatred, as in "You shall not hate your brother in your heart" (v. 17). Whereas Jesus regularly redefined civil law and fulfilled sacrificial and ceremonial law, He upheld and even intensified much of the moral law. For instance, Jesus describes His mission as one of "recovering . . . sight to the blind" (Luke 4:18) in accordance with Leviticus 19:14 and not only prohibits us from hating our brothers but even commands us to love our enemies (Matthew 5:43–47), a broadening of Leviticus 19:17. Jesus followed God's moral code. So should we.

Finally, the reason we do not abide by every Old Testament stipulation is because of the way we read the Bible. We read every law through the lens of what Christ taught, what He has done, and what He fulfilled (Matthew 5:17; Romans 10:4). He took the capital punishment of the civic law that all of us, as sinners, deserve when He died on the cross. He put an end to the sacrificial law by being the "better sacrifice" (Hebrews 9:23) in His death. And He lived a perfectly moral life in our stead so that we could be declared righteous in God's sight (2 Corinthians 5:21). To understand Old Testament law, we must understand it through Christ. He is our authoritative commentator on this law, so we live according to His interpretation of it and His teaching on it.

To dig deeper into how the Old Testament is read through the lens of Jesus Christ, read pp. 20–29 of Concordia Commentary: *Song of Songs* by Christopher Mitchell (CPH, 2001).

God gave Abraham's descendants many laws—civil, sacrificial, and moral. He also gave them many blessings—divine guidance, miracles, and food. All of these were meant to call the Israelites back from their grumbling to God's righteousness (Romans 2:4). But Israel did not stop complaining, so God sent the prophets to call her back again.

To dig deeper into the levitical laws and explore how they find their fulfillment in Christ, read the introduction of Concordia Commentary: *Leviticus* by John W. Kleinig (CPH, 2004), especially pp. 20–30.

N is for *Nebi'im*

I have a favorite prophecy, but it's not what you might expect. When many people think of prophecy, they think of Old Testament forecasts of a generous and forgiving Messiah. Isaiah 7:14 comes to mind: "The Lord Himself will give you a sign. Behold, the virgin shall conceive and bear a son, and shall call His name Immanuel." This one verse has led to countless Christmas songs, pageants, and sermons. But my favorite prophecy is nothing of this sort. It's Amos 4:1: "Hear this word, you cows of Bashan, who are on the mountain of Samaria, who oppress the poor, who crush the needy, who say to your husbands, 'Bring, that we may drink!' " Yes, the prophet Amos just called the women of Israel "cows." And no, I've never heard this prophecy sung in a song or acted out in a pageant. I have heard it preached, but only in a single sermon, and that pastor is now serving another congregation.

The reason I appreciate this prophecy so deeply is because it captures the profound burden that these preachers of old had to carry. The prophets had the tough-as-nails task of pointing out, sometimes with very colorful metaphors, Israel's sin and then calling her back to repentance, only to have that call rejected again and again. Elijah had to flee the wicked Jezebel, who hated him so much she wanted to kill him (1 Kings 19:1–8). Isaiah had to announce Israel's impending doom to King Ahab (Isaiah 7:17–25). And Jeremiah was so reviled that King Jehoiakim burned his prophecies (Jeremiah 36) and his own countrymen threw him into a cistern (38:1–6). Being a prophet was not a glamorous job.

Ultimately, even the now beloved prophecies of a Messiah were not well received, for the Messiah Himself was not well received. As Isaiah predicted of Christ, "He was despised and rejected by men; a man of sorrows, and acquainted with grief; and as one from whom men hide their faces He was despised, and we esteemed Him not" (53:3).

The recorded accounts of the prophets witness how they were rejected by the nation they were called by God to serve. The Messiah they foretold faired with no better treatment as He was rejected by the people He came to save. But their wicked rejection could not thwart God's gracious mission.

K **is for** *Ketubim*

In my kitchen, there is a drawer. Actually, there are many drawers. Some are filled with silverware. Some are filled with dishrags and potholders. But one particular drawer is filled with, well, everything. This drawer is the one into which stuff gets thrown when that stuff has nowhere else to go. Whisks. Apple corers. Spatulas. Matches. Birthday candles. You name it, it's in there. It's the catchall drawer.

In many ways, the books known as the Writings serve as the catchall drawer of the Old Testament. Whatever doesn't go in the Torah or the Nebi'im winds up in the Ketubim. What has landed in this catchall drawer? For starters, the Writings include the poetry of the Psalms and the wide range of human emotion they express—everything from joy to sorrow to anger. Consider these examples:

> My lips will shout for joy, when I sing praises to You;
> my soul also, which You have redeemed.
> (Psalm 71:23)

> My life is spent with sorrow, and my years with sighing;
> my strength fails because of my iniquity,
> and my bones waste away. (31:10)

> Be angry, and do not sin; ponder in your own hearts
> on your beds, and be silent. (4:4)

Luther loved the Psalms not only because of the wide range of emotions they expressed, but because of the synopsis of Scripture they offered and the Christ they confessed:

> The Psalter ought to be a dear and beloved book, if only because it promises Christ's death and resurrection so clearly and so depicts His kingdom and the condition and nature of all Christendom that we may well call it a little Bible. Most beautifully and briefly it embraces everything in the entire Bible.[1]

It is no wonder that the Psalms have been a source of hope, comfort, and strength for Christians over the millennia, for the Psalter picks up on the themes and promises of all of Scripture.

Next, the Writings offer wisdom from Proverbs, Ecclesiastes, and Job. In these books, we discover the source of wisdom is not ultimately learning or experience, but God Himself: "The fear of the LORD is the beginning of wisdom, and the knowledge of the Holy One is insight" (Proverbs 9:10). We also discover that wisdom is not only a quality to be acquired but a person to be trusted. In Proverbs 8, wisdom speaks: "I, wisdom, dwell with prudence, and I find knowledge and discretion. . . . The LORD possessed Me at the beginning of His work, the first of His acts of old. . . . When He established the heavens, I was there; when He drew a circle on the face of the deep" (vv. 12, 22, 27). This personification of wisdom finds its full expression in Christ, who is "the wisdom of God" (1 Corinthians 1:24).

Lastly, the Writings include many of the historical narratives of the Old Testament, from 1 and 2 Chronicles to Ruth and Esther to Ezra and Nehemiah, among others. These narratives chronicle the lives and times of Israel's kings, the people's spiral into sin, their exile from their homeland in an act of divine judgment, and their restoration to their land in a crescendo of divine grace. For a couple of different reasons, these historical narratives can be troubling to modern readers.

BORING

First, some readers find these historical narratives to be downright boring. As a pastor, I have been asked more than once, "Why does the Old Testament waste so much space on so many boring genealogies? Didn't God have more important things to reveal to us?" Take this account of King Saul's descendants:

In Gibeon lived the father of Gibeon, Jeiel, and the name of his wife was Maacah, and his firstborn son Abdon, then Zur, Kish, Baal, Ner, Nadab, Gedor, Ahio, Zechariah, and Mikloth; and Mikloth was the father of Shimeam; and these also lived opposite their kinsmen in Jerusalem, with their kinsmen. Ner fathered Kish, Kish fathered Saul, Saul fathered Jonathan, Malchi-shua, Abinadab, and Eshbaal. And the son of Jonathan was Merib-baal, and Merib-baal fathered Micah. The sons of Micah: Pithon, Melech, Tahrea, and Ahaz. And Ahaz fathered Jarah, and Jarah fathered Alemeth, Azmaveth, and Zimri. And Zimri fathered Moza. Moza fathered Binea, and Rephaiah was his son, Eleasah his son, Azel his son. Azel had six sons and these are their names: Azrikam, Bocheru, Ishmael, Sheariah, Obadiah, and Hanan; these were the sons of Azel. (1 Chronicles 9:35–44)

Be honest. Did you read every name, or did you just glance over these verses? Wading through who is related to whom and how many children there are, one can quickly get lost and bored. I especially love this genealogy because it's titled in the English Standard Version "Saul's Genealogy Repeated"—as if the first genealogy of Saul in 1 Chronicles 8 wasn't enough!

But we should not dismiss these genealogies. They set the stories of the Bible in real space and real time with real people, emphasizing Scripture's pedigree of historicity. They also remind us how God's love is active through the ages, from generation to generation. Each name in each genealogy is remembered and recorded by God because each name matters to God. Just like your name.

PUZZLING AND OFTEN CONFUSING

Another difficulty some people have with these historical narratives has to do with the actions God sometimes takes. What God does can catch you off guard! For instance, in 1 Chronicles 5, the Reubenites, the Gadites, and the half-tribe of Manasseh go to war. They win handily and carry off "50,000 . . . camels, 250,000 sheep, 2,000 donkeys, and 100,000 men" because "the war was of God" (1 Chronicles 5:21–22). Really? God wages war? God sanctions bloodshed and plunder? That doesn't seem right. The atheist evolutionist Richard Dawkins epitomizes the confusion of many when he writes:

> The God of the Old Testament is arguably the most unpleasant character in all fiction: jealous and proud of it; a petty, unjust, unforgiving control-freak; a vindictive, bloodthirsty ethnic cleanser; a misogynistic, homophobic, racist, infanticidal, genocidal, filicidal, pestilential, megalomaniacal, sadomasochistic, capriciously malevolent bully.[2]

God's actions can confuse us. Dawkins's opinion of God, however, does not. He lets us know precisely how he feels.

It's not just atheists who feel this way about what God does in the Old Testament. In the second century, there lived a bishop named Marcion. In his study of Scripture, Marcion found the Christ of the New Testament to be incompatible with the God of the Old Testament. He accordingly undertook to create his own version of Scripture, redacting anything from the Bible that, in his own opinion, smacked of Old Testament theology. His Bible included only one Gospel, Luke, and even this he heavily edited. He did not include Jesus' or John the Baptist's births, for these implied connections to things that came before—things from the Old Testament. He also omitted the genealogy of Luke 3:23–38, because of its lengthy list of Old Testament names, as well as the temptation narrative in Luke 4:1–13, because Jesus quotes from Deuteronomy to fend off Satan. If it was from the Old Testament, it was out. By his actions, Marcion put himself outside of the Christian faith. The Church condemned him as a heretic in AD 144.

DISTINGUISHING GOD'S WORK

In order to understand some of the more puzzling aspects of God's ways and works, especially in the Old Testament, we make a distinction between the two different ways God operates. Luther called these methods God's "alien work" and God's "proper work."[3] God's "alien work" is His wrath and judgment at sin and sinners, as the prophet Isaiah explains:

The LORD will rise up as on Mount Perazim;
as in the Valley of Gibeon He will be roused;
to do His deed—strange is His deed! And to
work His work—alien is His work! Now therefore do not scoff, lest your bonds be made
strong; for I have heard a decree of destruction
from the Lord GOD of hosts against the whole
land. (28:21–22)

God will sometimes use war, bloodshed, and catastro-
phe to judge sin and sinners according to His righteousness.
But this is not what God desires to do. Instead, God longs to
do His "proper work" of forgiveness and grace, as He Himself
declares, "Have I any pleasure in the death of the wicked, declares the Lord GOD, and not rather that he should turn from
his way and live?" (Ezekiel 18:23). God does both His alien and
proper works, but He delights only in one: His proper work
of mercy.

THE APOCRYPHA

No survey of the Old Testament would be complete
without at least a cursory word about the Apocrypha. Often-
times, when individuals from a Roman Catholic background
go through a new member class to join the congregation I
serve, they ask, "Why do Lutherans have fewer books in their
Bible than the Roman Catholics?" It is true. The Roman Catholic canon—that is, the collection of individual books that

make up the Bible—has seventy-three books while the Lutheran canon has only sixty-six books. The "extra" books are known as the Apocrypha.

The word *apocrypha* is related to a Greek term meaning "hidden" and describes a series of books written between the end of the Old Testament and the beginning of the New Testament, a period of approximately 430 years. Luther thought the books of the Apocrypha were important, calling them "useful and good to read,"[4] but did not consider them part of the canon of Scripture. Indeed, the Church never universally recognized these books. Jerome, a fifth-century doctor of theology, wrote, "The Church reads Judith, Tobit, and the books of Maccabees [books of the Apocrypha], but does not admit them among the canonical Scriptures. . . . [They do not] give authority to doctrines of the Church."[5] Jerome makes two important observations. First, he notes that though the books of the Apocrypha can be read, they are not to be considered canonical. Second, he explains that we are not to derive doctrine from these books, for, because these books are not divinely inspired, they can lead us into false teaching. This concern is perhaps best illustrated by 2 Maccabees 12:44–45, when the Jewish liberator Judas Maccabeus prays for some who have died, seeking to make atonement for the sins they committed while they were still alive. From this singular passage, the Roman Catholic Church derives its doctrine of purgatory, a place in which deceased believers undergo a final purification from sin that readies them for the bliss of heaven.[6] This runs contrary to the teaching of Scripture, which declares that a person enters either paradise or hell immediately upon death (e.g., Luke 16:19–31; 23:39–43).

The value of the Apocrypha lies primarily in the historical insight it gives into the period between the Old and New Testaments. It tells stories of Jewish faithfulness in the face of Hellenistic persecution, and it chronicles the origins of the religious parties, such as the Pharisees and Sadducees, that we meet in the New Testament. It is to this Testament that we will turn next.

To explore more about the place of the Apocrypha in Christian literature and the nature of the writings, read *The Apocrypha: The Lutheran Edition with Notes* (CPH, 2012), especially the introductory essays and materials.

Key Points

- The Old Testament is classically divided into the Law, the Prophets, and the Writings.

- The Law tells the origins of Israel and the world. It explains how sin entered creation and how God desires to bless the world in spite of its brokenness.

- Christ's teachings are our ultimate authority on the Law. He has met the Law's demands on our behalf.

- The prophets were sent to call God's people to repentance. They rebuked Israel's sinfulness, and comforted Israel with the promise of a Messiah.

- The Old Testament Writings are those not covered in the Law and the Prophets. They share praise, wisdom, and real stories of human failure and God's grace.

- Another group of books, the Apocrypha, contains useful history but is neither divinely inspired nor the source of doctrine.

Discussion Questions

1. What Old Testament books are most intimidating to you? Why? What do you think these intimidating books have to teach you?

2. Recently, there has been a string of newspaper and magazine articles criticizing Christians for upholding Old Testament standards for human sexuality (see Leviticus 18:1–23) while feeling free to jettison other Old Testament laws, such as the prohibition against eating shellfish (Leviticus 11:9–12). What is the difference between these two laws (see Matthew 19:5–6 and Acts 10:9–16 for help)? How does this highlight the importance of interpreting all laws through the lens of Christ?

3. Some people assume the primary job of a prophet is to foretell the future. What phrase comes up again and again in the following prophetic passages?

- Isaiah 41:14

- Jeremiah 2:29

- Ezekiel 16:14

- Haggai 1:13

4. How does this phrase help you understand the prophets' primary mission (see 2 Peter 1:21)? With this in mind, consider how each of these people are prophets:

- Jesus

- Your pastor

- You (see Acts 2:17–18)

5. Luther spoke of God's "alien work" and God's "proper work." How does this distinction both call you to repentance and comfort you? Does God ever damn those who turn from their sins (2 Chronicles 7:14)? As a believer, then, do you need to fear God's eternal wrath?

Action Items

1. Recall the books that you identified as "most intimidating" in the first question. Pick one of those intimidating books and challenge yourself to read it, using the notes of a study Bible or a commentary to help you.

2. Isaiah is crystal clear in his presentation of Christ some seven hundred years before His birth! Review the following passages, and consider these questions for each: (1) What period of Jesus' life and ministry is Isaiah describing? (2) Is there any New Testament language

that directly echoes Isaiah's language? (3) How can you use these prophecies to witness to someone who does not know or believe in Christ?

Isaiah 7:1–17

Isaiah 9:2–7

Isaiah 11:1–10

Isaiah 40:1–5

Isaiah 52:13–53:12

3. Write down your toughest question about one of God's actions in the Old Testament. Discuss it with your pastor in Bible class or one-on-one.

For all the days, weeks, and months that slip by with barely a notice, there is the occasional moment that becomes indelibly etched into our memories. Sometimes, the moment is tragic, like when we suffer the loss of a loved one. Other times, the moment is glorious, like when a baby, a child, is born. For me, an indelible moment came the day of my wedding.

It was a picture-perfect morning. There wasn't a cloud in the sky. The sun was shining. The birds were chirping. And it was a crisp 65 degrees outside—not bad for a December 30, even in San Antonio. My fiancée, Melody, and I had been planning for months, and now the morning was finally here.

Out of all the memorable moments of that morning, the one most precious to me is when I first saw my bride. Traditionally, the groom is not supposed to see his bride until she bursts through the back door of the sanctuary as the music rattles the rafters and the congregation rises to its feet. I, however, managed to catch a glimpse of my beloved a few seconds early.

The music had already begun, the groomsmen were awaiting their bridesmaids, and I stood ready to greet my soon-to-be wife. As I was looking toward the back of the sanctuary, waiting for her to enter, I caught a glimpse of her through the church's back windows, rushing down the breezeway to get into position for her grand entrance. That one glimpse took my breath away. I got weak in the knees and tingly to my toes. After all the planning, the preparation, and the organization, the moment had finally arrived—the moment when Melody and I would be joined by the Lord in His sight as husband and wife. And when I caught that first glimpse of my beautiful bride, I knew this moment was going to be a spectacular one.

God's Little Entrance

It took Melody and I many months to plan her big entrance through the backdoor of that sanctuary. It took God many millennia to plan His little entrance through the backwaters of our world. But God's entrance through Jesus into the hamlet of Bethlehem, as unassuming as it may have first appeared, has been indelibly etched into the annals of human history, for this moment was a spectacular one.

The apostle Paul writes of this moment, "But when the fullness of time had come, God sent forth His Son, born of woman, born under the law, to redeem those who were under the law, so that we might receive adoption as sons" (Galatians 4:4–5). This passage is one of my favorites. It reminds me that, for all the days, months, years, decades, centuries, and millennia that pass, time does more than march inexorably forward. Instead, time has a central moment, a pinnacle, if you will, It is the moment God sent forth His Son. This, Paul says, was the "fullness of time." It is as if time was pregnant and Jesus' arrival was nothing less than history giving birth to the reason it exists in the first place. All of history, there-fore, hinges on Jesus. Even the way we mark time reflects this. Before the fullness of time, we number our days using BC, meaning "Before Christ." Following the fullness of time, we number our days using AD, meaning "Anno Domini," Latin for "the year of our Lord." With Jesus, the calendar changed—and so did our world. And this change, this magnificent mo-ment, is recorded in the pages of the New Testament.

The New Testament may be divided into several parts.

THE GOSPELS, which record the birth, life, death, resurrection, and ascension of Jesus.

THE BOOK OF ACTS, which recounts the ministry and growth of the early Christian Church.

THE PAULINE EPISTLES, named for their author, the apostle Paul, which address major issues of doctrine and practice at various Christian churches scattered across Asia Minor and beyond.

THE CATHOLIC EPISTLES, which are not addressed to a specific congregation but are instead explicitly universal in their appeals.

Finally, **REVELATION**, a dazzling dissertation on Christ's rule and return.

As with the Old Testament, it is valuable to take a closer look at the component parts of the New Testament.

The Life and Times of Jesus of Nazareth

One of the glories of the Christian faith is that it is blessed with four reliable accounts of its founder's life and ministry: the accounts of Matthew, Mark, Luke, and John. These are the Gospels. Before we briefly survey each of these books, it is important to note that the term *gospel* may be used in a couple of different ways. On the one hand, it may refer to the records of Jesus' incarnated life and ministry. On the other hand, it may denote the good news "that Christ Jesus came into the world to save sinners" (1 Timothy 1:15). These two uses of *gospel* come together in the Gospels, for in these books, we read not only about the history of Jesus' life and ministry, but also about the purpose of Jesus' life and ministry: to save sinners. As Jesus says, "I did not come to judge the world but to save the world" (John 12:47). Jesus' history, then, cannot be divorced from Jesus' purpose. With this in mind, let's explore specific features of each Gospel and gain a fuller picture of our Savior.

THE GOSPEL OF MATTHEW

When Matthew wrote his Gospel, he seemed especially interested in relating Jesus' life and ministry to events and promises from the Old Testament. Indeed, one of the unique features of Matthew's Gospel is his continuous citing of Old Testament prophecies, explaining how they are fulfilled in Christ (e.g., 1:22–23; 4:14–16; 8:17; 21:4–5). Jesus' connection to what has come before Him is solid in Matthew's Gospel.

In this sense, Matthew reminds us that when Jesus enters history's stage, He is no one new, but an old promise of God who has taken on flesh and blood for us and for our salvation.

THE GOSPEL OF MARK

If Matthew's Gospel carefully and deliberately connects Jesus to the past of the Old Testament, Mark's Gospel jolts its reader back to the hustle and bustle of the present. Mark is often characterized as the "action Gospel," because in it Jesus is constantly on the move. Mark's favorite word is "immediately," which he uses forty-one times to rapidly shift the action from one account of Jesus to another. Even the end of this Gospel feels hurried. It is likely that Mark's Gospel should end with the women's terrified reaction to Jesus' resurrection: "They went out and fled from the tomb, for trembling and astonishment had seized them, and they said nothing to anyone, for they were afraid" (16:8). Many scholars believe that a scribe later added verses 9–20 to provide a more suitable and less abrupt ending to Mark. This is why modern translations of the Bible have a note explaining that Scripture's most ancient manuscripts do not have Mark 16:9–20.

THE GOSPEL OF LUKE

Luke is the studious historian of the four Gospel writers. The opening verses of Luke's Gospel point to the kind of careful research that has gone into his writing:

Inasmuch as many have undertaken to compile
a narrative of the things that have been accomplished among us, just as those who from the
beginning were eyewitnesses and ministers of
the word have delivered them to us, it seemed
good to me also, having followed all things closely
for some time past, to write an orderly account for
you, most excellent Theophilus, that you may have
certainty concerning the things you have been
taught. (1:1–4)

The Greek word for "certainty" in verse 4 is used else-
where in the New Testament to denote "security," as in 1 Thes-
salonians 5:3. Luke's contention is that he has meticulously
fact-checked everything in his Gospel. The reader, therefore,
can feel absolutely secure that what he or she reads really
happened. It is the truth!

As difficult as it is to search out sources, crosscheck
them, and compile them into a historical narrative, Luke
seems to enjoy the challenge. Luke's Gospel is only volume 1
of a historical *magnum opus*. Luke writes volume 2 when he
pens the Book of Acts:

In the first book, O Theophilus, I have dealt
with all that Jesus began to do and teach,
until the day when He was taken up, after He
had given commands through the Holy Spirit
to the apostles whom He had chosen. (Acts 1:1–2)

If Luke's Gospel is a history of Jesus' incarnated life and ministry, the Book of Acts is a history of the advent and spread of the Early Church. Notice, however, that Luke considers both of his volumes to be histories of Jesus. Luke says that his Gospel only "dealt with all that Jesus began to do and teach" (v. 1). Jesus' life, ministry, death, and resurrection were only the beginning. Throughout the Book of Acts, Jesus does many more things, though this time, instead of doing them with a small band of followers, He does them through His larger Church.

THE GOSPEL OF JOHN

Finally, we arrive at the Gospel of John. Whereas Matthew and Luke begin with Jesus' birth (Matthew 1:18–25; Luke 2:1–7) and Mark begins with John the Baptist inaugurating Jesus' public ministry (1:9–11), John begins a little further back: "In the beginning was the Word, and the Word was with God, and the Word was God. He was in the beginning with God. All things were made through Him, and without Him was not any thing made that was made" (1:1–3). In order to explain Jesus' origin, John begins not in the town of Bethlehem or with the appearing of John the Baptist, but at the beginning of creation itself. John argues that if Jesus was present at creation, He is no mere mortal, nor is He only vaguely divine. Rather, He is none other than God Almighty. In John's Gospel, Jesus testifies to His unity with God the Father in His words (8:48–58) and through a series of signs (2:1–11; 4:46–54;

11:38–44; 12:17–18). These signs, more than simple miracles, are meant to point to Jesus' unique position as God incarnate and to engender and strengthen faith in Him as such. Luther speaks of the value of divine signs:

> In all His promises, moreover, in addition to the word, God has usually given a sign, for the greater assurance and strengthening of our faith. Thus He gave Noah the sign of the rainbow. To Abraham He gave circumcision as a sign. To Gideon He gave the rain on the ground and on the fleece. So we constantly find in the Scriptures many of these signs, given along with the promises.[1]

To His people of old, God gave many signs that pointed to Him. To us He gives the sign of Jesus, who not only points to God but is God.

THE "LOST" "GOSPELS"

Over the past decade, a fury of interest has mounted over what are popularly referred to as the "lost" "Gospels." Both words deserve their own separate quotation marks because both are inaccurate.

The popular perception of the "lost" "Gospels" is that they were once contenders among a field of many for adoption by the Church as the truth about Jesus' life. The story goes that the Church, in an unabashed power grab, suppressed some Gospels that did not serve its political purposes, while officially adopting the ones we accept as part of the canon now—Matthew, Mark, Luke, and John—at the Council of Nicaea in AD 325. This popular perception of the rise of the New Testament canon is flatly false.

To begin with, issues of biblical canonicity were nowhere addressed in the decrees of the Council of Nicaea. It wasn't even part of the conversation. Second, by the time this Council was convened, the canon of the New Testament was already basically solidified. A list of New Testament books dating to about AD 170 closely corresponds to the books we have in our present-day canon.[2] This is why calling these "Gospels" lost is incorrect. The Christian Church has always known of their existence but has consistently rejected them—even well before the Council of Nicaea—because what these alternative Gospels teach is patently heretical and historically false. The end of the Gospel of Thomas, for instance, quotes Peter as saying that females are not worthy of life. Jesus responds to Peter's bravado by promising to make females male so they can enter His kingdom.[3] This example from Thomas serves to underscore why these so-called "Gospels" are not Gospels at all, at least in the traditional sense of the term. From the earliest times, they have been rejected because they don't speak of Jesus' life, death, or resurrection in any sort of historical context as the canonical Gospels do. Instead, these "lost Gospels," present Jesus as a disembodied sage, uttering pearls of wisdom mixed with bizarre teachings. Some went so far as to invent a Jesus and a Christianity that needed no cross for the atoning sacrifice for the forgiveness of sin.

Ultimately, the Church did not declare the four Gospels, or, for that matter, any other books of the New Testament to be canonical. Rather, the books of the Bible asserted themselves as canonical to the Church by means of their unimpeachable history and orthodox theology. As the Commission on Theology and Church Relations of The Lutheran Church—Missouri Synod explains:

> The Sacred Writings authenticated themselves by their inherent power to convince God's people that they are His Word. A biblical book did not become authentic because the Church accepted it; the Church accepted it because it was authentic and commended itself to the Church as an inspired, prophetic, or apostolic writing.[4]

The Bible commended itself by itself. No other book, save a truly inspired one, could do such a thing.

Sincerely, Paul

The New Testament consists of twenty-seven books. Of these, thirteen were written by one man: Paul. Actually, Paul's writings are not so much books as they are letters. Some are written to churches, such as Romans, 1 and 2 Corinthians, Galatians, Ephesians, and Philippians, while others are written to individuals, such as 1 and 2 Timothy, Titus, and Philemon.

But for all their unique features, these letters share a common credo: "Jesus Christ and Him crucified" (1 Corinthians 2:2). Paul's letters are all about Jesus.

Paul's resolute commitment to Christ is not surprising considering Paul's experience with Christ. In the Book of Acts, we learn that Paul, also called Saul, was making his way to Damascus on horseback to persecute Christians when suddenly a bright light from heaven flashed. He was knocked off his horse, and a voice from heaven asked, "Saul, Saul, why are you persecuting Me" (9:4)? The voice, it turns out, was the voice of the Lord. Christ commanded Saul to go to the house of Ananias, a prominent Christian, to be commissioned as God's "chosen instrument . . . to carry My name before the Gentiles and kings and the children of Israel" (v. 15). From this point forward, Saul, soon to be widely known as Paul, went from being an oppressor of Christians to an evangelist for Christianity.

Paul's spectacular encounter with the Lord informed His whole ministry. He never lost sight of the fact that it was God who called him and made him who he was. The openings of his letters show Paul's deep gratitude to God for His call:

> Paul, called by the will of God to be an apostle of Christ Jesus . . . (1 Corinthians 1:1)

> Paul, an apostle of Christ Jesus by the will of God . . . (2 Corinthians 1:1)

> Paul, an apostle of Christ Jesus by the will of God . . . (Ephesians 1:1)

> Paul, an apostle of Christ Jesus by the will of God . . .
> (Colossians 1:1)

Time and time again, Paul insists that his ministry is not the result of his own intellectual savvy, pious morality, or comprehensive strategy; rather, his ministry—indeed, his whole life in Christ—is thanks to God's will and grace. It is no surprise, then, that Paul would pen words such as these: "For by grace you have been saved through faith. And this is not your own doing; it is the gift of God, not a result of works, so that no one may boast" (Ephesians 2:8–9).

Paul didn't just write these verses as a theoretical theology, but as a living reality, for without God's grace for Paul's salvation, Paul couldn't have written about God's grace for humanity's salvation! Paul wasn't just writing about any salvation experience; Paul was writing about his salvation experience. And Paul's pervasive hope is that his salvation experience by grace through faith will be everyone's salvation experience, for it is the only true salvation experience there is.

All the Catholic without All the Rome

Along with Paul's letters, there are also the Catholic Epistles, which were written for the Church-at-large and are devoid of specific addressees. These letters include

> **Hebrews**, probably originally a Christian sermon on how levitical law is fulfilled in Christ's sacrifice on the cross;
>
> **James**, a treatise that closely echoes Jesus' Sermon on the Mount;

1 and 2 Peter, which speak extensively of Christian suffering;

1, 2, and 3 John, which herald the value and virtue of Christian love;

and **Jude**, which argues for the necessity of pure doctrine.

Though these letters are referred to as Catholic Epistles, this does not imply a connection to the Roman Catholic Church. The word *catholic* is from two Greek words: *kata*, a preposition meaning "according to," and *holikos*, meaning "whole." Thus, to be catholic means to be "according to the whole" or "universal." These letters are called catholic, then, because they were written for the whole Church.

Calling certain epistles catholic does not imply that Paul's letters lack universal appeal. Paul himself asserts the catholic character of his letters in places such as 1 Corinthians 1:2: "To the church of God that is in Corinth, to those sanctified in Christ Jesus, called to be saints together with all those who in every place call upon the name of our Lord Jesus Christ, both their Lord and ours." Paul writes not just to the congregation at Corinth, but to "all those who in every place" follow Christ. Likewise, at the end of Colossians, Paul offers this instruction: "When this letter has been read among you, have it also read in the church of the Laodiceans; and see that you also read the letter from Laodicea" (4:16). Paul wanted his letters to be read, studied, and exchanged between many congregations, benefiting and blessing the entire Church.

A Dragon and Horsemen and Beasts, Oh My!

No survey of the New Testament would be complete without a word of explanation concerning what is perhaps Scripture's most befuddling and challenging book: Revelation. Many people have tried to understand this apocalyptic tour de force, and many have failed. A quick read through Revelation uncovers everything from a dragon to horsemen to beasts, oh my! Just how does one read such an unusual book?

To understand the vision given to John that is recorded in Revelation, we must begin with a fundamental question: "What did John have in mind when he wrote this book?" Failing to ask this question can lead to wild interpretations that distort John's intentions and message. For instance, when I was in high school, I was a member of a Christian club. Once a week, we met during lunch for Bible study. I can still remember one session on the infamous mark of the beast, 666 (Revelation 13:18). The Bible study leader theorized that the mark of the beast was secretly being coded onto computer chips that the government would soon implant into our foreheads to turn us into lobotomized Satanists. It was heavy stuff. But it also was completely false. This conspiratorial interpretation doesn't take into account John's cultural context and concerns. Earlier in the chapter, John notes that the beast who bears this mark has "two horns like a lamb," but it speaks "like a dragon" (13:11). Thus, this beast, though it tries to masquerade as the Lamb of God, really works for Satan. The number of this beast bears this out. In apocalyptic numerology, seven is the number of perfection. Three is the number of the Trinity. Three sixes exemplify this beast's charade: he wants to appear as God Himself, who is perfect and triune, but he always falls short. He can never make it to a perfect seven.

The mark of the beast as a computer chip and other fantastical interpretations Revelation's numbers and metaphors create fear concerning the second coming of Christ rather than faith. People are terrified of a day that will bring nothing but gloom and gore. But John says the Last Day will explode with glory and gladness as God eliminates sin and its ill effects once and for all:

> "He will wipe away every tear from their eyes, and death shall be no more, neither shall there be mourning, nor crying, nor pain anymore, for the former things have passed away." And He who was seated on the throne said, "Behold, I am making all things new." (21:4–5)

The Bible's closing book teaches us about the time when Christ will return—the time when He will wipe away all tears, death, mourning, and pain. When Christ returns, He will replace gloom and gore with glory and gladness. When Christ returns, He will make everything new—including you.

Key Points

- The word *gospel* may refer to Christ's sacrifice for our salvation or to the four New Testament accounts—

Matthew, Mark, Luke, and John—of Christ's life and His purpose: to save sinners.

- Each Gospel has a unique perspective that join to form a well-rounded picture of Christ. They highlight His fulfillment of Old Testament prophecies (Matthew), His miracles and travels (Mark), His life researched from outside sources (Luke), and His divine origin (John).

- The Church has always known about and consistently rejected the so-called "lost" "Gospels" due to their historical and theological inaccuracies.

- Paul wrote thirteen of the twenty-seven New Testament books and emphasized the Gospel of salvation by grace through faith.

- The Catholic Epistles are the letters written by people other than Paul. They are named for the Greek word *catholic*, meaning "universal," since they were written for the Church-at-large.

- For Christians, Revelation should not be a terrifying apocalyptic picture, but a comforting promise that when Christ returns, sin, death, and the devil will be destroyed forever.

Discussion Questions

1. Jesus changed the course of history. He even left His mark on our calendar: our years are now divided into BC (Before Christ) and AD (*Anno Domini*, Latin for "the

year of our Lord"). What are some other ways Jesus has changed the course of human events and thinking? How does Jesus' history-shifting work bolster the Christian confession of faith about who He is?

2. Why do you think the Gospel writers provide us with different perspectives on Jesus' life? How do these perspectives complement rather than contradict one another?

3. The New Testament is made up of many letters—both the letters of Paul and the Catholic Epistles. How do these letters give us insight not only into what Jesus did but also into *why* Jesus did it? Why is understanding the purpose behind Jesus' actions so important (1 Timothy 1:15–16)? What happens if someone does not understand Jesus' purpose (Matthew 16:21–23)?

4. What are some of the theories you've heard concerning the end of the world? How have you seen Christ's coming portrayed in books or on TV? Do these books and movies accurately depict what the Bible teaches? Why or why not? Analyze these popular portrayals of the end of the world in light of Jesus' admonition to John to "fear not" (Revelation 1:17).

Action Items

1. Review the different emphases of the four Gospels. Pick which emphasis you'd like to learn more about, and read the corresponding Gospel.

2. Just like Paul found his identity in Christ, you should too. How should Christ inform your identity in . . .

    . . . your priorities?

    . . . your body image?

    . . . your relational interactions?

3. Do you need to make a change in any of these areas to better center your identity on Christ? Ask your spouse or a trusted friend to encourage and support you as you make a change.

4. Write down your toughest question about Jesus' life and ministry. Discuss it with your pastor in Bible class or one-on-one.

Confession is good for the soul, so here it goes: I am a tech snob. Specifically, I am an Apple tech snob. People sometimes refer to those who use Apple products to the exclusion of other tech toys as "Apple evangelists." I suppose you could count me among the converted. I read on my iPad. I watch shows using my Apple TV. I am typing this book on my MacBook Pro. And, of course, I own and have tethered to me at all times the ubiquitous iPhone.

When it comes to the iPhone especially, I can't help myself. Every time a new one comes out, I feel compelled to swap my old phone for the new one. After all, new iPhones come with new features. From higher resolution cameras to faster processors to more accurate voice controls, every new iPhone turns out to be better than the last. This is part of Apple's marketing genius. This is why whenever a new iPhone is released, reporters chronicle lines at Apple stores that stretch far into the streets, each person waiting with baited breath to hold Apple's latest technological marvel. It's because when Apple releases a new product, it's never just new, it's also improved.

New and Improved

> If anyone is in Christ, he is a new creation. The old has passed away; behold, the new has come. (2 Corinthians 5:17)

The promise of the Gospel is that Christ, through His Word, makes us new—and with newness in Christ comes definite improvement. When we are baptized into Christ, we go from death and damnation to life and salvation (Romans 6:4). That seems like a monumental improvement. When the Spirit indwells us, working in us and on us, we go from rebellion and wickedness to obedience and sanctification (Galatians 5:16–17). That's pretty impressive as well. When God's Word is preached to us, we are moved from darkness and depravity to light and revelation (Romans 1:21–23; 3:21–24). That, too, is nothing short of spectacular. God, through His Word, makes us new and improved, and this is a blessed thing. For apart from God's Word, we are old and broken.

Old and Broken

Scripture is clear: we are old and broken, even from the moment of conception. King David writes, "Behold, I was brought forth in iniquity, and in sin did my mother conceive me" (Psalm 51:5). Our default state, the psalmist says, is sinfulness. We confess this sad truth in worship when we say, "Most merciful God, we confess that we are by nature sinful and unclean. We have sinned against You in thought, word, and deed" (*LSB*, p. 151). In every way imaginable, we are old and broken. But God does not want to leave us this way. So He works through His Word to make us new and improved— in our thoughts, in our words, and in our deeds.

GOD'S WORD CAN MAKE US
NEW AND IMPROVED IN OUR THOUGHTS

God's Word can transform our minds. Jesus highlights the importance of our minds when He cites one of Israel's most beloved Bible verses: "You shall love the LORD your God with all your heart and with all your soul and with all your might" (Deuteronomy 6:5). Jesus amends this verse, adding, "You shall love the Lord your God with all your heart and with all your soul and with all your strength and with all your mind" (Luke 10:27). Jesus cares about our minds. The apostle Paul writes in a similar vein: "Finally, brothers, whatever is true, whatever is honorable, whatever is just, whatever is pure, whatever is lovely, whatever is commendable, if there is any excellence, if there is anything worthy of praise, think about these things" (Philippians 4:8). What goes through our minds matters.

The Bible teaches us many good things to think about and believe. These teachings are called doctrines. Unfortunately, *doctrine* has become a dirty word among many. I remember a lady at a church I once served who proudly announced to me one day that she hated doctrine. "Doctrine divides," she explained. "It divides Lutherans from Baptists and Presbyterians from Catholics. Love unites! We need to stop worrying about doctrine and just start loving each other." Though I certainly have no quibble with loving one another, I have to question this woman's blanket hatred of doctrine. Still, it is true that doctrine can divide. Jesus says as much:

Do not think that I have come to bring peace
to the earth. I have not come to bring peace,
but a sword. For I have come to set a man against
his father, and a daughter against her mother,
and a daughter-in-law against her mother-in-law.
And a person's enemies will be those of his own
household. (Matthew 10:34–36)

Jesus' teaching can divide people and even families. But
this does not make doctrine itself evil. Quite the contrary.
Doctrine wipes away the dusty uncertainties about the things
that matter most and gives us insight into the very mind
of God. The doctrine of justification by grace through faith
teaches how we are saved. The doctrine of Christ's incarnation comforts us with the promise that God is not distant and
aloof, but is as near as Jesus Christ. The biblical doctrines of
Baptism and the Lord's Supper tell us how Christ meets us
today—through water and the Word and with His own body
and blood. What a person has been taught and believes is
of inestimable consequence. It is no wonder that Paul wrote
to Timothy about the crucial significance of true doctrine:
"If anyone teaches a different doctrine and does not agree
with the sound words of our Lord Jesus Christ and the teaching that accords with godliness, he is puffed up with conceit
and understands nothing" (1 Timothy 6:3–4). Through true
doctrine, God makes our minds new and improved. It is well
worth our while, then, to briefly review some of the major
doctrines of the Bible.

JUSTIFICATION. The doctrine of justification is chief among all Christian doctrines. The Lutheran Confessions summarize this doctrine nicely:

> Our churches teach that people cannot be justified before God by their own strength, merits, or works. People are freely justified for Christ's sake, through faith, when they believe that they are received into favor and that their sins are forgiven for Christ's sake. By His death, Christ made satisfaction for our sins. God counts this faith for righteousness in His sight. (Augsburg Confession IV 3)

The doctrine of justification reminds us that our righteousness is not the product of our own morality, piety, or strivings, but a sheer gift from God, bestowed on us when Christ took our sin upon Himself on the cross and exchanged it for His righteousness. As Paul explains, "For our sake [God] made Him to be sin who knew no sin, so that in Him we might become the righteousness of God" (2 Corinthians 5:21).

SANCTIFICATION. The doctrine of sanctification is the inevitable outcome of the doctrine of justification. For when Christ bestows on us His righteousness, we cannot help but begin to act righteously. Paul describes such righteous acts this way: "The fruit of the Spirit is love, joy, peace, patience, kindness, goodness, faithfulness, gentleness, self-control; against such things there is no law" (Galatians 5:22–23). This fruit does not make us righteous in God's sight. Rather, the Spirit produces such fruit in us and through us because we have already been made righteous by Christ. Christ's righteous work always precedes our righteous fruit.

CREATION. The doctrine of creation provides us with three important reminders.

First, it reminds us of our origin. It tells us that we are "fearfully and wonderfully made" (Psalm 139:14) and not just a random collusion of atoms through which neurons fire for a time, only to dissolve back into the components parts from which they came.

Second, this doctrine reminds us of our position in creation. God has placed us as stewards over His creation. This is why God commands, "Fill the earth and subdue it, and have dominion over the fish of the sea and over the birds of the heavens and over every living thing that moves on the earth" (Genesis 1:28).

Third, this doctrine reminds us of our purpose. God's purpose for us is eternal. This is why before the fall, people did not die. Death was never a part of God's creative design but was a result of sin. In this way the doctrine of creation gives context to the doctrine of justification, for through justification, God forgives sins and grants eternal life.

We learn from the doctrine of creation that eternal life was God's design and desire for us from the very beginning.

INCARNATION. The doctrine of the incarnation comforts us with the promise of God's closeness through Christ. Because of sin, humans are by nature and by choice separated from God. In Christ, however, God comes near to sinful humans and draws them to Himself.

Paul explains, "In Christ Jesus you who once were far off have been brought near by the blood of Christ" (Ephesians 2:13). There is a breathtaking illustration of this on the ceiling of the Sistine Chapel. Michelangelo's famed fresco, *The Creation of Adam*, took the artist four years of intense labor to complete, pushing him to his physical limits. In it, God is portrayed as a white-bearded patriarch, straining to touch Adam's finger. Every muscle in God's arm is flexed. His finger is taut. Adam, on the other hand, appears much more ambivalent about the prospect of reaching out to God. He is reclining lazily on a patch of green with his finger hanging limply. The doctrine of the incarnation reminds us that even though Adam and all humanity would not reach out to God because of our sinfulness and rebellion, God reached out to Adam and all humanity through Christ.[1] Rather than remaining secluded in a shroud of holiness, God came near to us and took on our sinful plight in Christ.

SACRAMENTS. The doctrines of Baptism and the Lord's Supper are close corollaries to the doctrine of the incarnation. Through these Sacraments God continues to draw close to humanity, delivering Christ's forgiving and saving work through water connected to the Word in Baptism and through Christ's very body and blood in, with, and under the bread and wine of the Lord's Supper. Lutheran Christians regularly refer to these Sacraments as Means of Grace. But what exactly are Means of Grace?

When I was a freshman in college, I did not have a car. So when it came to meals, I was stuck eating in the college cafeteria. But the cafeteria fare got real old real quick. I wanted something better even though I had

EXPECT TO BE MADE NEW

no vehicle. Thankfully, I could call and get a Mr. Gatti's pizza delivered. I could not get to good food, so Mr. Gatti's delivery ensured that good food could come to me. This is what Christ does through the Means of Grace. We have no vehicle to get to Christ and His forgiveness and salvation. No rocket can take us to Jesus in heaven, nor can we travel back in the time to the cross. Instead, Scripture teaches us that through the Sacraments, Christ brings His forgiveness and salvation to us. The Sacraments are delivery vehicles by which God gets His grace to human beings.

ESCHATOLOGY. The doctrine of eschatology refers to those things that will take place upon Christ's return. Indeed, the word *eschatology* means "last things." The promise of this doctrine is that God's desire to be with us—as exemplified in the incarnation and the Sacraments—will reach its full and final goal upon Christ's return. John envisions the breathtaking scene like this: "The dwelling place of God is with man. He will dwell with them, and they will be His people, and God Himself will be with them as their God" (Revelation 21:3). The Last Day will bring the closest of communions with God—and it will bring it forever.

This is, of course, just a core sampling of the many doctrines taught in the Bible. As Christians, we are called to study and learn these and other doctrines, for they are knowledge from God that can be used by God to form and strengthen faith. Apart from the foundation these doctrines provide, we will be left adrift in a sea of uncertainty and relativism, unable to distinguish the truth of divine revelation from the many falsehoods of this world. So take doctrine seriously. Your thoughts are sure to be made new and improved by it.

GOD'S WORD CAN MAKE US NEW AND IMPROVED IN OUR WORDS

Words have power. Just ask anyone who has ever received a compliment after a bad day. Just ask anyone who has ever had to endure a vicious verbal attack from an enemy. In the first instance, a bad day can turn good because of a single word of affirmation. In the latter case, a good day can turn bad as a person replays rough words over and over. This is why James, the leader of the Church in Jerusalem, cautions us to choose and use our words wisely: "Know this, my beloved brothers: let every person be quick to hear, slow to speak, slow to anger" (James 1:19). Though James's admonition is simple and straightforward, it is nevertheless humanly impossible. He himself admits this: "Every kind of beast and bird, of reptile and sea creature, can be tamed and has been tamed by mankind, but no human being can tame the tongue. It is a restless evil, full of deadly poison" (3:7–8). The tongue is so powerful it cannot be tamed by any human. It wags as it pleases and can do terrible damage to those it spites.

If the human tongue has such tremendous power for good or for ill, imagine the power of God's tongue!

The psalmist marvels, "By the word of the LORD the heavens were made, and by the breath of His mouth all their host. . . . For He spoke, and it came to be; He commanded, and it stood firm" (Psalm 33:6, 9). God spoke. The world happened. Such is the awesome authority of God's tongue and God's Word.

The preacher of Hebrews says, "For the word of God is living and active, sharper than any two-edged sword, piercing to the division of soul and of spirit, of joints and of marrow, and discerning the thoughts and intentions of the heart" (4:12). Notice all the things God's Word can do. It can pierce a person's soul, calling forth repentance and faith. It can burrow its way into a person's heart, pricking the conscience and guiding morals. There is no limit to the abundant power of God's Word.

Words have tremendous power. Thus, it is critical that our words come under the authority of God's Word so they can be used as God intended: as vehicles that carry the truth about human sin and the good news about divine grace. Paul outlines how we should speak to one another: "Having put away falsehood, let each one of you speak the truth with his neighbor, for we are members one of another" (Ephesians 4:25). Interestingly, the Greek word for the preposition "with" in this passage is ambiguous. In some English translations, it is rendered as "to." This ambiguity in the original Greek actually serves to accent the fullness of Christians speaking. At times, we are called to speak truth "to" the people in our lives—using words of the Law to call them to repentance from their sin and using words of the Gospel to comfort them when they are sorrowful over sin. Other times, we are called to speak truth "with" our neighbors; that is, we are called to confess with them our common faith. We do this in worship when we speak together the creeds or pray together the Lord's Prayer or sing together the great songs of the Church. Christian speech involves both speaking "to" each other so we can hear the truth and speaking "with" each other so we are reminded that, together, we share the truth.

Our speaking should also include spreading the Gospel to those whose words and hearts have not yet been brought under the authority of God's Word and love. As Paul explains, "Walk in wisdom toward outsiders, making the best use of the time. Let your speech always be gracious, seasoned with salt, so that you may know how you ought to answer each person" (Colossians 4:5–6). Our words ought to be vigorously employed in service to God's mission of reaching lost people.

GOD'S WORD CAN MAKE US NEW AND IMPROVED IN OUR DEEDS

A transformed mind and mouth inevitably lead to transformed hands that act on what the mind thinks and the mouth speaks. God's Word is not given to us so we can merely ponder it deeply or speak it eloquently. God's Word is given to us so we can do what it says faithfully! The Bible is replete with admonitions to do what it says:

> Everyone then who hears these words of Mine and
> does them will be like a wise man who built
> his house on the rock. (Matthew 7:24)

If you know these things, blessed are you if you do them.
(John 13:17)

Be doers of the word, and not hearers only,
deceiving yourselves. (James 1:22)

Scripture is meant to transform our deeds. This does not, however, mean that our deeds become perfect when we believe God's Word. Indeed, James's admonition, "Be doers of the word," is perhaps better translated, "Become doers of the word." We are all growing in doing God's Word. No one heeds God's voice perfectly. But God's Spirit can sanctify us and enable us to do what we cannot do on our own. That reminds us of the most important reason God's Word is given to us: to work faith within us. This faith, then, results naturally in action.

Paul, in his letters, puts special emphasis on doing God's Word. Each of Paul's letters includes a section of *paraenesis*, a Greek word meaning "exhortation." In his exhortations, Paul admonishes his believing readers to godly living, putting into practice the Scriptures they have learned. Such *paraenesis* is grounded in what Lutheran Christians call "the third use of the Law." Whereas the first use of the Law is meant to restrain evil and evildoers and the second use of the Law condemns and convicts sinners, the third use of the Law serves as a guide, showing a Christian how to walk in paths of righteousness. The Lutheran Confessions summarize the third use of the Law:

Although believers are regenerate and renewed in the spirit of their mind, in the present life this regeneration and renewal is not complete. It is only begun.... It is necessary that the Law of the Lord always shine before them, so that they may not start self-willed and self-created forms of serving God drawn from human devotion. (Epitome VI 4)

According to the Lutheran Confessions, Christians must have the guide of God's Law to tell them what actually pleases the Lord. Otherwise, they will invent all sorts of works that may seem noble on the surface but are really just moralistic tripe. This understanding and use of God's Law undergirds what Paul seeks to do as he exhorts his readers. Rather than leaving his readers to live according to the shaky and shadowy stirrings of their own imaginations, he outlines for them how to live according to the sure and certain standard of God's revealed will.

Paul's exhortations of Christians toward God-pleasing deeds take on different forms. Sometimes, it is a list of vices and virtues, contrasting righteousness with wickedness to highlight the importance of a sanctified character:

> To learn more about the third use of the Law see Martin Luther's disputation Against the Antinomians. The text is found in Luther's Works, vol. 47, with a new translation in vol. 61. See also a discussion of the disputation in *Friends of the Law* by Edward Engelbrecht (Concordia, 2011), 147–62.

Put to death therefore what is earthly in you: sexual immorality, impurity, passion, evil desire, and covetousness, which is idolatry.... Put on then, as God's chosen ones, holy and beloved, compassionate hearts, kindness, humility, meekness, and patience, bearing with one another and, if one has a complaint against another, forgiving each other; as the Lord has forgiven you, so you also must forgive. And above all these put on love, which binds everything together in perfect harmony. (Colossians 3:5, 12–14)

Paul's language of "putting on" godly virtues is noticeably baptismal, echoing Paul's picture of Baptism in Galatians 3:27: "For as many of you as were baptized into Christ have put on Christ." The apostle's assertion is that in putting on Christ through Baptism, one should also put on a Christlike character and gladly live as Christ commands.

Paul's exhortations can also take the form of how a household should be ordered. For instance, in the case of husbands and wives, he says the following:

Wives, submit to your own husbands, as to the Lord. For the husband is the head of the wife even as Christ is the head of the church, His body, and is Himself its Savior.... Husbands, love your wives, as Christ loved the church and gave Himself up for her, that He might sanctify her, having cleansed her by the washing of water with the word. (Ephesians 5:22–23, 25–26)

These domestic codes are meant to be practical, covering everything from how spouses relate to each other to how parents relate to their children. They even extend outside the home to how employees relate to their employers (Ephesians 6:1–9). Such a focus on order in the household and in society-at-large reflects the character of our God, who is "not a God of confusion but of peace" (1 Corinthians 14:33).

Lastly, Paul's exhortations can address a number of "hot topics" happening in the lives of his readers. In 1 Corinthians, Paul explicitly addresses some of the hot topics of the Corinthian Christians, even beginning with these words: "Now concerning the matters about which you wrote" (7:1). Apparently, the Corinthians wrote Paul with several questions. Paul, in turn, provides answers on everything from marriage (ch. 7) to how to celebrate the Lord's Supper (11:17–24) to how to exercise spiritual gifts (chs. 12, 14). These eerily echo the same concerns we have in our day. Thus, a study of Paul's instruction is important for any Christian to undertake, for the issues he addresses are the same ones we deal with today.

We are born old and broken. Jesus, however, wants to make us new and improved. Such a transformation of our old thoughts, old words, and old deeds began at Baptism and is continuously fueled by God's Word. So, actively feed these changes with God's Word. And remember, even as you go through many changes—some happy, some sad, and some even downright painful—you are being changed by a God who Himself is unchanging. After all, He has no need to change. He's perfect. Anchor your changes in Him, and know that your salvation does not rely on your changes but on the faithfulness of our unchanging God.

Key Points

- We sin against God by nature and by choice, "in thought, word, and deed." Christ rescues us from sin and makes us new through His Word.

- God's Word can make us new in our thoughts. God wants us to devote our minds to righteousness rather than to wickedness. This can be done by studying Christian doctrine.

- Understanding biblical doctrines is critical to appreciating God's work for us and among us. Two key doctrines are justification and sanctification:

  Justification teaches that we are saved not by our own works, but by Christ's work on the cross, by which He gives us His righteousness.

  Sanctification reminds us that as recipients of the righteousness of Christ we are empowered by the Holy Spirit to live according to God's Word and will.

- Other core doctrines are creation, which shares our origin from God; incarnation, which teaches about God's Son becoming human; Baptism and the Lord's Supper, through which we receive God's gifts; and eschatology, which teaches us to joyfully await Christ's return.

- God's powerful Word can make us new in our words. We are called to use our words in accordance with God's perfect and holy Word.

- God's Word can make us new in our deeds. His Word shows us how to walk in righteousness.

- Paul's letters include exhortations on how to live. These speak to vices and Christian virtues, Christian households, and other hot topics of doctrine and practice.

Discussion Questions

1. God's Word can make you new in your thoughts! What role does doctrine play in your everyday thinking about God? What would you say to another Christian who tells you, "Doctrine is bad because it divides people"?

2. God's Word can make you new in your words! Think about the words you use. Consider how you can use them either sinfully or righteously in . . .

   . . . your household.

   . . . your workplace.

   . . . the political arena.

   . . . the entertainment industry.

   . . . your church.

3. When someone uses hurtful words against you, how can you best respond?

4. God's Word can make you new in your deeds! The Bible teaches that your deeds cannot save you (Ephesians 2:8). Why, then, are deeds still important (Luke 10:30–37)?

Action Items

1. Take some time to confess before God how you have sinned against Him and others in thought, word, and deed. Ask for God's forgiveness through Christ.

2. Develop an action plan! What can you do this week to . . .

    . . . learn more about one of the doctrines covered in this chapter?

    . . . affirm a loved one with gracious words?

    . . . bless someone with a kind deed?

3. Write down your toughest question about Christian doctrine. Discuss it with your pastor in Bible class or one-on-one.

I used to work as a DJ at a country radio station in Austin and, later, in Corpus Christi. I am a big fan of country music, so it was a kind of dream job for me to get paid to read up on all the latest Nashville gossip, share tidbits from the lives of country stars, and play song after song.

Even though I've been out of the business for some time, radio still holds a special place in my heart. So you can imagine my delight when, a while back, I was asked to appear as a guest on a nationally syndicated radio show. The host of the show had stumbled across my weekly blog and wanted me to share some of what I had written with his audience. I eagerly accepted his invitation. After all, what could be better than making a triumphant return to the airwaves, even if it was only for an interview?

I quickly realized, however, that this interview wasn't going to be what I had anticipated. The host skipped the opening pleasantries so he could launch directly into a series of combative questions. "So," he began, "did you go to school to be a pastor, or were you called by God?" I answered with a simple "yes." After bantering back and forth about whether or not formal education is vital to ministry formation, he finally protested, "I just don't understand why you need seminary training to teach you how to understand the Bible when the Spirit lives inside of you. He should be all you need!"

You Light Up My Life

The antagonistic radio host had this much right: we cannot fully understand Holy Scripture apart from the Holy Spirit. The Spirit lights up our lives—and our minds. Paul explains, "No one comprehends the thoughts of God except the Spirit of God. Now we have received not the spirit of the world, but the Spirit who is from God, that we might understand the things freely given us by God" (1 Corinthians 2:11–12; see also 2 Corinthians 4:4–6). Luther says likewise, "If God does not open and explain Holy Writ, no one can understand it; it will remain a closed book, enveloped in darkness."[1] The Spirit must rule our minds in order for us to truly appreciate the splendor and significance of Scripture. Still, just because we highly value the Spirit's illumination doesn't mean our own sinful natures don't get in the way. Left unchecked, our sinfulness obscures and perverts what the Spirit seeks to teach.

Paul writes about the effect humanity's sinful state has on people's understanding of the divine: "They are darkened in their understanding, alienated from the life of God because of the ignorance that is in them, due to their hardness of heart" (Ephesians 4:18). A hard heart darkens the mind to the things of God. The Scriptures are full of examples of this. Shortly after Jesus miraculously multiplies five loaves of bread and two fish and passes it to His disciples to share with five thousand hungry mouths, Mark notes, "They did not understand about the loaves, but their hearts were hardened" (Mark 6:52). The disciples' hard hearts darken their minds to the things of God. Shortly after Jesus raises Lazarus from the dead to the amazement of the multitudes, John writes, "Though [Jesus] had done so many signs before them, they still did not believe in Him, so that the word spoken by the prophet Isaiah might be fulfilled: . . . 'He has blinded their eyes and hardened their heart' " (John 12:37–38, 40). A hard heart darkens the mind to the things of God.

It's not just that people's hearts are hardened to the teachings of Jesus, it's that people's hearts are hardened to all of Scripture. Peter says of Paul's writings, "There are some things in them that are hard to understand, which the ignorant and unstable twist to their own destruction, as they do the other Scriptures" (2 Peter 3:16). People reject Paul's letters just like they reject Jesus' teachings. Their hard hearts darken their minds to the things of God, and apart from the illumination of the Spirit, their minds will remain darkened. For only the Spirit can light up our minds to the wonders of God's Word.

Interpret Alone at Your Own Risk

The Church has long believed that as the Spirit lights up our minds to the beauty of the Bible, He does so in the context of community. The study of Scripture is not meant to be a solitary hobby but a joint endeavor. A seminary professor of mine, James Voelz, notes that biblical interpretation should be done "by a believing Christian within a Christian community in accordance with the creedal understanding of those

Scriptures by the historic Christian Church."[2] In other words, one should not attempt to interpret the Bible alone!

The Scriptures themselves testify to the importance of studying the Bible with others. When God gives Israel His Word through Moses, He says, "These words that I command you today shall be on your heart. You shall teach them diligently to your children, and shall talk of them when you sit in your house, and when you walk by the way, and when you lie down, and when you rise" (Deuteronomy 6:6–7). God wants what He commands in His Word to be talked about in families, taught to children, and discussed with others out on the open roads. What is the common denominator in these scenarios? Community! God wants people to study His Word in community. And what was true for Israel is also true for the Church. The plural pronoun of Acts 2:42 makes this clear: "They devoted themselves to the apostles' teaching and the fellowship, to the breaking of bread and the prayers." In this verse, the pronoun "they" refers to the community of the Church. The "apostles' teaching" is nothing other than Scripture's teaching. Thus, in Acts 2, the community of the Church was together studying scriptural teaching.

As the Church has studied Scripture together, it has arrived at some short and memorable synopses of Scripture's teachings known as creeds. Three of these creeds are called "ecumenical," that is, they are held in common by all those who are Christian. The three ecumenical creeds are the Apostles', Nicene, and Athanasian Creeds. These soaring summaries of Scripture are sometimes referred to as the *regula fidei*, a Latin phrase meaning the "rule of faith," a term first coined by the Church Father Tertullian around AD 200.

> With regard to this rule of faith . . . it is, you must know, that which prescribes the belief that there is one God, and that He is none other than the Creator of the world, who produced all things out of nothing through His own Word, first of all sent forth; that this Word is called His Son . . . at last brought down by the Spirit and power of the Father into the Virgin Mary, was made flesh in her womb, and, being born of her, went forth as Jesus Christ . . . having been crucified, He rose again the third day; having ascended into the heavens, He sat at the right hand of the Father; sent instead of Himself the power of the Holy Ghost to lead such as believe; will come with glory to take the saints to the enjoyment of everlasting life and of the heavenly promises, and to condemn the wicked to everlasting fire, after the resurrection of both these classes shall have happened, together with the restoration of their flesh.[3]

Tertullian's rule of faith sounds strikingly similar to what Christians today confess in the Apostles' Creed. The rule of faith, then, has not changed over the millennia. It has always been what the Christian Church believes, teaches, and confesses because it is what Scripture believes, teaches, and confesses.

Scriptural interpretation is to be done inside the boundaries of the rule of faith. As Voelz notes in the quote at the beginning of this section, any interpretation of Scripture should be checked against "the creedal understanding of those Scriptures." Though theologians are at liberty to search for shades of meaning in various Greek and Hebrew words, to put forth their best arguments for the precise year of Jesus' birth, or to debate whether Mark or Matthew was the first Gospel written, they are not free to stray outside the rule of faith. To do so is to depart from the Church's consensus understanding of the core of biblical teaching and thereby to reject the foundation of the Christian faith. As one of my seminary professors put it, "The creeds are vitally important because they keep you from getting weird." Don't be weird and interpret the Bible as a lone ranger. Draw gladly from the wisdom of the creeds. After all, the creeds were asking and answering big spiritual questions long before you were. Learn from them.

> Along with the creeds, there are many other people and resources that can help you understand and interpret the Bible better. Here are a few of them.

YOUR PASTOR. Your pastor is called by God to help you grow in your understanding of Scripture. This is why he crafts sermons and prepares Bible studies. As a pastor myself, I receive all sorts of questions about the Bible, ranging from questions on the meaning of a Bible passage to the biblical basis for a particular doctrine to why people experience trials or tribulations. I delight in helping people answer their questions so that they can better apply God's Word to their lives. Your pastor will too. Don't hesitate to talk with him.

THE DOCTORS OF THE CHURCH. From the ancient Church Fathers to today's theologians, the trained and learned in the Church can yield you awe-inspiring insights into the teachings of Scripture. In this book, I have quoted Clement of Rome, Tertullian, and, of course, the Lutheran Confessions and Martin Luther. I also cited one of my seminary professors. In my research for this book, I consulted many other well-regarded theologians as well, checking my writing against their insights. Why? Because I would be a fool not to take advantage of the wealth of insight bequeathed to me by the larger Christian Church. The teaching of others has helped me understand Scripture in a way that I would never have been able to if I just studied Scripture on my own. These great minds of the Church can help you too.

CHRISTIAN FRIENDS. Your Christian friends can help you grow in your understanding of Scripture. Sometimes, a friend can share just the right scriptural insight at just the right time. When you are hurting, a friend might offer comfort from Psalms: "I waited patiently for the LORD; He inclined to me and heard my cry" (40:1). When you are joyful, a Christian brother or sister might celebrate with you according to the scriptural admonition to "rejoice with those who rejoice" (Romans 12:15). When you have a question in a small group Bible study, another participant may have the very answer you've long been looking for. It's not just professional theologians who have insight into the Bible; everyday Christians do too! Joyfully learn from the wisdom of these people, because, so often, it is born out of deep interaction with Scripture in times of study and personal need and deep integration of Scripture into their daily lives.

RESOURCES. Scripturally faithful resources can help you understand the Bible better. This book aims to be one such resource. There are many others out there as well. Study Bibles with their notes, charts, and maps can prove immensely valuable. They can succinctly answer many of the common questions a person has while reading the Bible. All you have to do is glance at the notes at the bottom of the page. Commentaries on Scripture are also helpful. A wealth of in-depth insights can be gained from theologians who have carefully studied the biblical texts in their original languages while also paying attention to the historical and cultural settings of Scripture. It should be noted that there are both "professional commentaries," which are published with theologians and pastors in mind, and commentaries expressly written for people with limited biblical knowledge. Search out the commentaries that are right for you. You won't regret it.

A word of caution is in order when it comes to the people and resources cited above. Because humans are sinful, they can and do sometimes err. Some pastors have been known to teach false doctrine, even publishing it in best-selling Christian books. The doctors of the Church, as wonderfully insightful as they may be, can sometimes depart from clear scriptural teaching. The third-century Church Father Origen, for instance, taught that, ultimately, all would be saved, even if they did not trust in Christ in this life. The Church father Tertullian criticized the Baptism of children. These teachings are not in line with Holy Scripture. Likewise, while your friends can sometimes offer much needed comfort from Scripture, they can at other times offer guidance that—though it may sound vaguely Christian in its sentiment—is misleading or even downright incorrect. I can remember during a time I was struggling when a friend tried to comfort me by saying, "The Bible says, 'God won't give you more than you can handle.' " The Bible says no such thing. God gives people more than they can handle all the time. The biblical promise is not one of ease, but that of God's power, which is made perfect in our weakness (2 Corinthians 12:9). The watchword, therefore, as you consult different people and resources, is discernment. Even the wisest teachers can misspeak. Check and double-check what you hear, what you read, and the advice you are given against the only thing that is sure and certain: Holy Scripture itself.

A Note on Bible Translations

You're almost ready. You know that Scripture stars Jesus Christ. You know the broad story of the Old and New Testaments. You know that God's Word can and should make you new and improved. And you have your pastor on speed dial just in case you get confused. But there's still one final question to consider: which Bible translation should you use? After all, there are hundreds of Bibles out there. Which one is right for you? Before picking a Bible, it is helpful to know a little bit about different Bible translations and the philosophies that shape them.

Formal equivalence translations seek to translate the ancient Hebrew, Aramaic, and Greek of the biblical text word-for-word into English as far as possible. These translations can sometimes be difficult to read since the syntax and sentence structure of the biblical languages can vary widely from that of English. Examples of formal equivalence translations include the English Standard Version (ESV), the New American Standard Bible (NASB), and the King James Version (KJV).

Dynamic equivalence translations take phrases or even sentences from the original languages of the biblical text and try to translate them according to the intent of the biblical authors using smooth, readable English. These types of translations are often referred to as thought-for-thought translations in order to distinguish them from the word-for-word philosophy of the formal equivalence translations. Examples of dynamic equivalence translations include the New International Version 1984 and 2011 (NIV) and the New Living Translation (NLT).

Paraphrases consult other English translations of the Bible, as well as some Greek, Aramaic, and Hebrew texts, and then recast these resources into contemporary English. Examples of paraphrases include The Message (MSG) and the Good News Bible (GNB).

Every translation has its strengths and weaknesses. Dynamic equivalence translations, for instance, may be somewhat easier to read, especially for a biblical novice, but they make some translational decisions, as in the case of the NIV 2011, which are at best misleading and at worst grammatically and theologically in error.

Paraphrases are especially dangerous because they often explicitly, and sometimes even recklessly, reflect the theological biases of their paraphrasers, thereby convoluting and controverting the Bible's message. Generally, it is advisable to stay away from paraphrases. Formal equivalence translations, though they may be more difficult to read, follow the biblical text most closely and offer the most precise peek in English into what the ancient authors wrote in the original biblical languages. Most congregations of The Lutheran Church—Missouri Synod use either the ESV or the NIV 1984 in their worship and Bible studies.

For an important analysis of the weaknesses of the NIV 2011, see the "CTCR Staff Opinion on Inclusive Language in the New International Version (2011)" from the Commission on Theology and Church Relations of The Lutheran Church—Missouri Synod.

Everyone needs help reading and studying the Bible, so make liberal use of all the helps listed above. Remember also that, along with human help, God promises His divine help: "The unfolding of Your words gives light; it imparts understanding to the simple" (Psalm 119:130). God can lead you to a better, deeper, fuller understanding of His Word, even if you've only just begun to read it.

Key Points

- Apart from the Holy Spirit, we cannot truly understand the Holy Scriptures.

- A collective consensus forged among many over time tends to provide a stronger biblical interpretation than individual interpretations.

- The collective consensus of the Bible's high points is in the ecumenical creeds: the Apostles', Nicene, and Athanasian. The phrase "rule of faith" describes how these creeds norm and distinguish orthodoxy from heresy.

- Along with the creeds, other people and resources can help you interpret the Bible better. All must be checked for error against the sure and certain standard of God's Holy Word.

- When studying the Bible, a good translation is key. The main types are word-for-word translations, thought-for-thought translations, and paraphrases, which recast the Bible into easy-to-read English.

Discussion Questions

1. Consider what Luther says about the Spirit's work: "I believe that I cannot by my own reason or strength believe in Jesus Christ, my Lord, or come to Him; but the Holy Spirit has called me by the Gospel, enlightened me with His gifts, sanctified and kept me in the true faith" (SC II Third Article). How does Luther's statement shed light on the necessity of the Spirit's ministry as you read the Bible?

2. Even with the Spirit's work in your heart, your own sinfulness sometimes prevents you from correctly interpreting Scripture. Is there anything the Bible teaches that makes you uncomfortable? Have you ever tried to either ignore or rationalize this clear teaching of Scripture because of your own sinfulness? How?

3. Read the three ecumenical creeds. These can be found in *Lutheran Service Book*, pages 158–59 and 319–20, or online at www.lcms.org. Consider:

   What are the differences between each of the creeds?

   What are the concerns of each of the creeds?

   What does each of the creeds teach you about the Bible?

Action Items

1. Are you a part of a Bible study? If not, join one so that you can learn and study the Bible in the context of a community. If you are a part of a Bible study, invite a friend to join you!

2. Read a formal equivalence translation alongside a dynamic equivalence translation of the Bible. What differences do you notice? Are any of them especially significant? How can different translations of the Bible shed light on the text and on one another? If a difference in the translations confuses you, make sure to consult your pastor.

ASK FOR HELP

3. There are many resources that can help you interpret the Bible better! Discuss with your pastor either in Bible class or one-on-one what resources he recommends.

92

When I wake up, I hit the ground running

. . . literally. Every morning, I roll out of bed and head outside to pound the pavement before the sun comes up. It's a great way to begin my day. It gets my blood flowing and my head clear so I can tackle the day's challenges. I also spend time in prayer as I huff and puff down the road. In this way, my run serves as a sacred start to my day.

I used to be overweight. My blood pressure and cholesterol were through the roof. I knew I needed to make a change. I needed to change my eating habits, yes, but I also needed to exercise. Still, I could never seem to find the time. I was always too busy, too tired, or too sickly. I knew that if I was going to start exercising and keep exercising, I wasn't going to be able to just find the time. I never had any. Instead, I was going to have to make the time. So I did. I started waking up early to go running—at 4 a.m. I've been running ever since.

When I first started running, I couldn't even make it a mile. I would run out of breath. I would be drenched in sweat. I developed painful shin splints. It wasn't pretty. But thanks to changing my diet and pushing through my often-agonizing 4 a.m. runs, I slowly started to shed pounds and develop stamina. I began barely able to make it a half a mile. After a few months, I finally made it to a mile. Then I made it to two. These days, I run a 5k every day. I'm still not a long-distance runner, but even this relatively short run has changed my life.

I'm healthier than I have been in a long time, But it took some time to get here.

Making changes in your diet and exercise routine can be difficult. Reading the Bible can be difficult too. I remember a teacher telling me, "Bible study is hard work! But it's worth it." These words are most certainly true. Bible study is hard work. It takes intentionality. Indeed, if you want to read the Bible daily, it takes more than squeezing it in when you can find the time. You have to make the time regularly to be in God's Word. Moreover, even after you set aside that time, you may not make it very far—at least at first. You may set out with a plan to make it through three chapters only to wind up making it through three verses. That's okay. Start slow. Deal with the difficult passages of the Bible head on. And through it all, remember God's assurance that, by the Spirit's power, when you think on what Scripture says, "The Lord will give you understanding in everything" (2 Timothy 2:7).

Bible study is hard work! But it's worth it. God promises to fulfill His purpose for you as you read His Word. God says, "[My Word] shall not return to Me empty, but it shall accomplish that which I purpose, and shall succeed in the thing for which I sent it" (Isaiah 55:11). What is God's purpose in sending you His Word? It is so that you may know of—and believe in—the forgiveness of sins, life, and salvation given you through Christ.

So what are you waiting for? Put down this book and pick up God's book. It's a great read.

Introduction

1. Adam Nicolson, "The Bible of King James," *National Geographic* (December 2011), http://ngm.nationalgeographic.com/2011/12/king-james-bible/nicolson-text.

Chapter 1

1. Ewald M. Plass, ed., *What Luther Says: A Practical In-Home Anthology for the Active Christian* (St. Louis: Concordia, 1959), § 439.

2. Clement of Rome, "The First Epistle of Clement to the Corinthians," in *The Ante-Nicene Fathers.* A. Roberts, J. Donaldson, and A. C. Coxe, eds. (Buffalo: Christian Literature Company, 1885), 1:18.

3. *What Luther Says* § 174.

4. C. F. W. Walther, *Law & Gospel: How to Read and Apply the Bible*, trans. Christian C. Tiews (St. Louis: Concordia, 2010), 2 (Thesis I).

Chapter 2

1. Ewald M. Plass, ed., *What Luther Says: A Practical In-Home Anthology for the Active Christian* (St. Louis: Concordia, 1959), § 3167.

2. Richard Dawkins, *The God Delusion* (New York City: Houghton Mifflin Harcourt Publishing Company, 2006), 51.

3. See Thesis 4 of "The Heidelberg Disputation" in Martin Luther, *Luther's Works*, vol. 31, J. J. Pelikan, H. C. Oswald & H. T. Lehmann, eds. (Philadelphia: Fortress Press, 1957), 44.

4. *Luther's Works*, vol. 35, J.J. Pelikan, H.C. Oswald & H.T. Lehmann, eds. (Philadelphia: Fortress Press, 1960), 337.

5. Jerome, "Prefaces to the Books of the Vulgate Version of the Old Testament," *A Select Library of the Nicene and Post-Nicene Fathers of the Christian Church, Second Series*, vol. VI, P. Schaff & H. Wace, eds. (New York: Christian Literature Company, 1893), 492.

6. See *Catechism of the Catholic Church* (Collegeville: The Liturgical Press, 1994), 268–69.

Chapter 3

1. Martin Luther, *Luther's Works*, vol. 35, J. J. Pelikan, H. C. Oswald & H. T. Lehmann, eds. (Philadelphia: Fortress Press, 1960), 86.

2. The "list" is found in the Muratorian Fragment. For a fine overview, see F. F. Bruce, *The Canon of Scripture*, (Downers Grove: InterVarsity Press, 1988), 158–69.

3. The Gospel According to Thomas 114.

4. "The Inspiration of Scripture," A Report of the Commission on Theology and Church Relations of The Lutheran Church—Missouri Synod (March 1975), http://www.lcms.org/Document.fdoc?src=lcm&id=302.

Chapter 4

1. This illustration is based on one by John Ortberg, *God Is Closer Than You Think* (Grand Rapids: Zondervan, 2005), 1–4.

Chapter 5

1. Martin Luther, *Luther's Works*, vol. 13, J. J. Pelikan, H. C. Oswald & H. T. Lehmann, eds. (St. Louis: Concordia Publishing House, 1956), 13.

2. James W. Voelz, *What Does This Mean? Principles of Biblical Interpretation in the Post-Modern World*, 2nd ed. (St. Louis: Concordia Publishing House, 1995), 229.

3. Tertullian, "The Prescription Against Heretics," *The Ante-Nicene Fathers*, vol. 3, A. Roberts, J. Donaldson & A. C. Coxe, eds. (Buffalo: Christian Literature Company, 1885), 249.